Cradle

to

College

Cradle
to
College

by
Brannon Howse

New Leaf Press

First Edition

ISBN: 0-89221-243-8
Library of Congress Catalog Number: 93-86325

Dedication

To Melissa, my wife and the love of my life. Thank you for your patience with me while I was writing this book. For the many nights which we stayed home instead of going out. For the nights in which I bolted down your wonderful cooking only to return to the computer. For the many weekends you have traveled with me, sitting through the same sermon, the same concert, the same seminar, and still telling me how much you enjoyed each one and how you were looking forward to the next weekend because we would be together. I certainly married out of my league.

To my mom, who is always clipping articles from the newspaper and various magazines, helping to keep me informed on what is going on. For the many hours you spent helping me learn to read and write, two skills that were mandatory in the compiling of this book. For teaching me phonics when the local public school would not because they thought their way was better. For tutoring me every school night at the kitchen table all through my elementary years — even during the summer months, which I hated. You knew it was necessary if I was to ever overcome my dyslexia — and thanks to you, I did. For giving me my love for the old hymns at a very early age by singing them with me all the way to school each morning. For being honest and telling me the things that I need to hear, when I need to hear them.

To my twin sister Heather. You were my best friend until I met and married Melissa. Now you are my second best friend.

I will always remember the good times we had double dating through high school and the nights we rushed home to beat curfew. Also the many mornings in which you came out of your room dressed for school, and I came out of mine, only to see the other standing there wearing the same color shirt, the same color sweater, and your skirt being the same color as my slacks. Your response to this very common and unplanned behavior was the same response you would give when we said or thought the same thing. "It's because we're twins." You were probably right, and I am glad we are.

Acknowledgements

I would like to thank my wife, Melissa, for all her support and encouragement in all that I do.

A special thank you to my editor Val Cindric, a former teacher herself, whose deep committment to truth and the things of which I wrote in this book made her a real joy to work with.

To my mom and dad who instilled in me the values and commitment that I have for faith and family.

Contents

Preface

I am not about to say, "All that is wrong in America today is a result of a failed educational system." Parents and families must take responsibility for their own children.

The increasing and troubling problem is that the state, government, and school system are now fighting to take that responsibility from parents. Many of today's liberals and educational elite are doing everything they can through curriculum, classes, and legislation to undermine parental authority and responsibility, thus creating a wedge between the parent and the child.

I do not desire through this book to aid in the destruction of the public school system, but merely to help create a better, more productive, traditional, and balanced educational system. A system that strives to and is capable of accomplishing the purpose for which it was created — the education of our children and not the indoctrination of our children.

Aristotle wrote, "All who have meditated on the art of governing mankind are convinced that the fate of empires depends on the education of youth."

That's why I desire to see America filled with the best public schools, private schools, and home schools in the world. Schools that are free from massive state and government control. Schools where the parents are the ones with the power — the power to choose. To choose not only *what* their kids will be taught but *by whom.*

Martin Luther, writing centuries ago, had the same goal and shared the same fears:

I'm much afraid that schools will prove to be

great gates of hell unless they diligently labor in explaining the Holy Scriptures, engraving them in the hearts of youth. I advise no one to place his child where the Scriptures do not reign paramount. Every institution in which men are not increasingly occupied with the Word of God must become corrupt.

I envision a system that would allow you to send your child to the best public, private, or home school available. It would put the power and control of today's educational system where it rightfully belongs — in the hands of those who have the most sincere vested interest — the child's parents. Accomplishing such a task will not be easy, but it can be done if we commit ourselves to that which is truly important.

William Bennett, in his book *The Devaluing of America,* tells the story of Clare Boothe Luce and her visit with President John F. Kennedy at the White House.

She sat down and straightforwardly said, "Mr. President, you must get the Soviets out of this hemisphere." They talked a few minutes. Then the phone rang, and the president went off.

He came back rather excited and said, "I got my textile bill passed. What were you saying, Clare?"

Replied Mrs. Luce, "Mr. President, there are many great men remembered in our civilization. Of one man, they said He went to a cross and died so that all men's sins may be forgiven. Of another man, they said he went in search of a new route to an old world, and founded a new world. Of another it is said that he took up arms against his mother country and with a motley army of rebels defeated the greatest military power on earth to found a new nation. And of another, it is said that he had to hide in the dark of night as he came into

Washington, and grieved for four years that the nation might be half slave and half free. Mr. President, of none of these great men was it said, "He got his textile bill passed."

The time has come for us to realize what is truly important and then to fight for it. Will you be remembered as someone who had the big house, the expensive car, the cabin on the lake, and all the right name-brand clothes? Or will you be remembered as someone who was truly committed to that which was really important and eternal?

To be remembered for that which is temporal would mean I had failed at life. To be remembered for my love and commitment to Christ as well as my wife, family, and country is to be remembered for that which is eternal and truly important.

If you believe in the traditional family, the traditional Judeo-Christian faith, the United States of America, and the values through which it was made great, stand firm and fight for its preservation.

Ronald Reagan challenges us with these words: "Today more than ever, it is essential that . . . each of us remember that the strength of our family is vital to the strength of our nation." Our nation was founded on moral principles and standards. Take away these standards and principles, and America becomes nothing more than a seven-letter word.

In the chapters that follow, we will look at the present condition of education in America, the cultural and spiritual threats to the American family — and America herself.

May the contents of this book encourage you to either join or continue on in the fight for America and the traditional family in its quest for survival. Keep the faith, and remember, I read the end and WE WIN!

— Brannon Howse

1

America 2000: A Womb to Tomb Plan

"Such a school would probably start with babies and go through the eighth grade. It would be all year long. It would be open from 6 a.m. to 6 p.m."[1]

This shocking statement made by Lamar Alexander, secretary of education during the Bush Administration, reveals the educational elite's agenda for your children.

"But that will never happen," you say. Don't fool yourself. The plan is already in the works with "America 2000," a "break the mold" approach to education.

America 2000's goal is to replace the "traditional" way of teaching and make major changes in our current educational system. It seeks to nationalize educational goals, achievement tests, school assessments, and vocational training. This national education program will be a "womb to tomb" plan.

Although America 2000 has some admirable objectives, the dangers of this program far outweigh any of its benefits. Here are the six national educational goals that the United States Department of Education hopes to accomplish by the year 2000:[2]

1. All children in America will start school ready to learn.
2. The high school graduation rate will increase to at least 90 percent.
3. American students will leave grades fourth, eighth, and twelfth having demonstrated competency in challenging subject matter including English, mathematics, science, history, and geography; and every school in America will ensure that all students learn to use their minds well, so they may be prepared for responsible citizenship, further learning, and productive employment in our modern economy.
4. U.S. students will be first in the world in science and mathematics achievement.
5. Every adult American will be literate and will possess the knowledge and skills necessary to compete in a global economy and exercise the rights and responsibilities of citizenship.
6. Every school in America will be free of drugs and violence and will offer a disciplined environment conducive to learning.

These goals sound pretty good, don't they? But let's look closer at some of the actual objectives.

The first part of goal Number Three sounds valid, but the second phase, which reads, ". . . all students learn to use their minds well, so they may be prepared for responsible citizenship, further learning, and productive employment in our modern economy," allows for the implementation of a value based, non-cognitive educational program and standard. This program, known as Outcome Based Education, is already being forced on many school districts across the nation. The dangers of OBE will be addressed in a later chapter.

Ironically, Goal Number Four, which is to make American students first in the world in science and mathematics, will never be achieved with programs like America 2000 and Outcome Based Education. Instead, U.S. students will be first in nothing but stupidity.

Why 2000?

Why America 2000? Because the primary objective is to accomplish the six national goals, previously listed, by the year 2000.

The first step? To have 535 America 2000 schools by 1996 — this means one America 2000 school for every congressional district. By the year 2000, they propose to have all 110,000 elementary and secondary schools transformed over to the national standards.

Legislation was introduced in Congress allowing for a million dollar grant to be given to the first 535 schools to demonstrate a plan that would "break the mold." This legislation was tabled. As a result, the New American Schools Development Corporation, a nonprofit corporation, was formed.

The purpose of this corporation is to underwrite the program by giving several grants a year to those schools who submit the best "break the mold" proposal. The funds for these grants come from many large and small companies who are interested in the nationalization of education. You might ask, "Why would American business be interested in nationalizing education?"

American business understands first-hand the problem of a failing educational system because they are having a hard time finding qualified employees. For example, "Motorola found that an appalling four-fifths of those seeking employment could not pass a test of seventh-grade English and fifth-grade math. New York Telephone had 117,000 job applicants in 1988, but could find only 2,100 who could pass the company's employment test."[3]

Many corporations are supporting America 2000 because they truly believe that through government control, the educational system will greatly improve. Could there also be a monetary motive? It's been suggested that a better educated populace would flood the job market with *over-qualified* employees, thus driving down wages and making available cheap labor for hire.

Whether or not they receive a grant from the New American School Corporation, many school officials have declared that they are going through with their "break the mold" plan. But is America 2000, the way to do it?

In the several school districts presently run by the federal government, studies have shown that the students in these schools fall a year to a year and a half behind students in non-government run public schools. Apparently, America 2000 is striving to do on a national level what the government has already failed to do on a small scale.

John Chubb and Terry Moe, authors of *Politics, Markets & America's School,* have "documented the educational consequences of bureaucratic 'interference' with school management." What were their findings? Schools where boards of education, city councils, or other political bodies heavily influenced daily management and curricular decisions of principals turn out students who are more than a year behind their peers in what the authors termed an "effective school." They found that parental choice and market competition were the keys to creating these effective schools.[4]

No matter how much data we provide proving that parental choice creates better schools, the liberals and educational elite shove the statistics aside. Why? It's not because they don't believe the numbers; it's because they know we are right. You see, when it comes to a choice between doing what is best for you and your kids and promoting themselves and their cause, you and your kids are the losers every time.

One-Stop Child Care

Phyllis Schlafly, president and founder of Eagle Forum, notes that America 2000 has a concept that "includes expanding the public schools in order to 'parent' children through their pre-school hours and to provide non-school services." How do they plan to do this? According to Schlafly:

America 2000 wants to transform public schools into baby sitters for pre-kindergarten kids, and into social service centers to provide meals, health care (probably including the controversial kinds), counseling, and guidance. [5]

In a speech at the Kansas Governor's Summit on Education in 1989, Secretary of Education Lamar Alexander made it clear that he favors making schools "one-stop shopping" centers for the dispensing of family planning, health care, and social services.

America 2000's goal is to place everything a child needs within the four walls of the school. As a result, the schools will become a type of "proxy" parent. In fact, the promoters of this program make it a selling point that the school will become the center of the community. Wait a minute! What ever happened to the idea that the family was the center of the community?

The center of the community once was the town square where families visited, played, and shopped. As the size of our towns and cities grew, the center of the community became the block on which we lived. Mothers and fathers sat outside on warm summer evenings sipping a cool drink, watching the sun go down while neighbors worked in their yards and kids rode bikes up and down the street. This was the center of the community.

As kids, we learned about life not only from our parents but also from our friends' parents who would not hesitate to grab us by the back of the shirt and chew us out for misbehaving. They would then march us home, still holding the back of the shirt, and present us to Mom, who would then take her turn in the disciplinary process.

This was the center of the community, where parents raised their kids with the values of respecting God and country. A place where wrong was wrong and right was right, and you were not rewarded for doing right, because it was expected of you.

Today our schools do not tell kids they have the wrong

answers, much less what is right and wrong. After all, every-thing is relative, and what is truth to me may not be truth to you; and what is truth today, may not be truth tomorrow.

Instilling Values Not Knowledge

According to Phyllis Schlafly, the national testing that America 2000 calls for "will inevitably prescribe a national curriculum."[6] Believe me, this national curriculum will be less about academic achievement or cognitive knowledge and more about attitudes and values — and it most certainly will not be the traditional Judeo-Christian values upon which this country was founded.

It is at this point that America 2000 and Outcome Based Education coincide. Outcome Based Education will promote nothing less than political correctness.

Chester Finn, author of *We Must Take Charge,* and former assistant secretary of education, trumpets the benefits of a national curriculum. He argues that since kids all over the country eat the same Big Macs and watch the same "Ninja Turtles" TV shows, there is little cause for concern in having them study the same core curriculum.[7]

A popular theme of school curriculum today, which is being used nationwide, is what *Newsweek* has called, "The Curse of Self-Esteem." We spend so much time trying to make the student feel good about himself, we leave little time for him to educate himself — which would actually be the surest way to promote his self-esteem.

Phyllis Schlafly has said,

> The folly of this fad was best illustrated by the comic strip kid who told his stuffed animal pal, "I quit doing homework, homework is bad for my self-esteem. It sends the message that I don't know enough. Instead of trying to learn, I'm just concentrating on liking myself the way I am." To the question as to how his self-esteem could be "enhanced by remaining an ignoramus" the child

replies, "Just call me informationally impaired."
Maybe that's the name of a new "disability" that
will entitle the kid to a job under the Americans
with Disability Act. [8]

With all its vague objectives, America 2000 allows for
the implementation of Outcome Based Education, along with
other such mindless programs that guarantee a lot of fluff and
very little substance.

More Money!

Many support America 2000 because it will provide more
federal funding for education, thus improving the educational
system. Money, however, does not necessarily increase learning.

Years ago, most children were taught in the old one-room
school. These schools were operated on a shoe string budget
and without much more than a blackboard and chalk. This
simple educational system produced students like George
Washington, the father of our country; Abraham Lincoln,
author of the Gettysburg Address, the man who freed the
slaves, and founded the Republican party; and Laura Ingalls
Wilder, one of America's best-loved authors who wrote the
Little House on the Prairie books, which later became one of
the most successful and popular series in American television
history. In fact, in a recent *TV Guide* survey Americans voted
"Little House on the Prairie," their favorite television series.

"But," some argue, "times have changed. Schools require
more money in order to be effective in today's sophisticated
world."

Okay, let's look at New York's School District Three.
Located on the fashionable West Side of Manhattan, District
Three is one of the wealthiest communities in the world and
provides its students with the best equipment and newest
textbooks. Out of 734 school districts in New York, District
Three ranks 734 in academic performance![9]

Steven Marshall of Bound Brook, New Jersey, proves the

point that more money does not equal better education:

> The fundamental problem with American education today is not lack of money; we do not under spend, we under produce. A review of some 150 studies shows no correlation between spending and educational achievement. In 1990 we spent $414 billion on education, roughly $140 billion more than on national defense. In absolute terms we spend more on education than any other nation in the world. John Silber, the president of Boston University, has written, "It is troubling that this nearly four-fold increase in real spending has brought no improvement. It is scandalous that it has not prevented substantial decline."
>
> Throwing money at problems has never solved anything. If it did, we would have the most well-educated young people in the world. Instead we spend an average of $6,000 a year per student in this country in 1992. Let's run the numbers on that $6,000.
>
> The average class size is what, thirty students? So 30 times $6,000 = $180,000 per classroom. The teacher probably earns around $30,000, so that leaves $150,000. Next we have books, chalk, utilities, building amortization, dead frogs, spit ball removers, school buses, drivers, school board members, principals, condoms, abortion counseling, attendants to valet park students' cars, and computers. Remember that we are spending $180,000 per classroom.
>
> How many classrooms are there in your neighborhood school? I'll bet we could do all the above plus hire college professors and pay them $50,000 per year and limo students to and from school every day and still have money left over. So just where is all that money going? What are

we getting for it other than a bunch of whiners who alternately demand and grovel for more every year? Think about that.[10]

It is a proven fact that our government spends more on education than on national defense. Money is not the problem. Unless educators get serious about changing America's educational philosophy, throwing more money at the problem will never lead to academic improvement. Educators need to commit themselves to educating — not indoctrinating.

Indoctrination takes time and money, and the only result will continue to be academic decline and lower test scores.

William Buckley, in a recent editorial, proves this point with these statistics:

> In 1945, public-school spending per pupil was $974 (all dollar figures here given are in 1992, i.e., constant dollars). In 1992, spending per pupil had risen to $5,216. Teachers' salaries in 1945 averaged $14,770, and by 1992 had risen to $35,334. How splendid! Five times as much spent on students, 2.5 times as much on teachers.
>
> The result? In 1950, SAT math scores were 493; in 1992, down to 476. In 1950, SAT verbal scores were 470; in 1992, 423. With results of that kind, one's reaction, is quite simply, instrumental. You fire the coach. [11]

Common sense would, indeed, tell us to fire the coach! But who should do the firing? The owners of the team, right?

Who owns the schools where student performance continues to decline? You do. Who pays the salaries of the administrators and teachers who keep producing a losing team? You — the taxpayers! Who elects school board members to their positions? You — the voters!

Parents, grandparents, and business people should work together to remove school board members who side with administrators and oppose the wishes of taxpaying parents. It's time for a change!

If you don't act now, it may soon be too late. Once America 2000 is in place, parents and local school boards will lose any control they now have over curriculum decisions. As a result, the coach will have more power than the owners, and the team will remain in last place.

Americanized Socialism

Although they call it America 2000, this program is definitely not very American. In fact, it will put the federal government in control of national education and promote nothing less than socialism. That doesn't sound too American to me.

Why do I make that statement? Because I know who's pushing America 2000.

Is it the parents and teachers who are involved day to day basis with the children of America? Is it the local school boards who are elected to represent the best interests of parents and students? Or is it the politicians in Washington who want to use America's children to achieve some global and social objective?

The prime sponsor of America 2000 is Senator Ted Kennedy, whose liberal philosophy revolves around socializing our democratic, capitalistic society. That should give you a clue as to the hidden agenda of this "educational" program.

Until the late 1970s, America had no bureaucratic Washington elites telling the people how to run their schools and classrooms. Then, under the Carter Administration the federal government organized the U.S. Department of Education.

A few years later, Ronald Reagan, while running for president, promised to abolish the Department of Education. President Reagan felt, like many other Americans, that the federal government should not be involved in the business of administering education and that this right and power belongs to people at the local level.

Although this was a noble objective, President Reagan

discovered it was an almost impossible task to accomplish. That's true of any government program once it gets a foothold in Washington. It would take a majority vote by Congress to abolish the massive Department of Education, and a vote against it would appear to be a vote against education in general. No congressman wants that vote on his record, regardless of the fact that it would be in the best interest of our nation's educational system.

Conform or Pay the Price

America 2000 will put the federal government in the drivers seat when it comes to education. But who needs the federal government? If they cannot run a two-bit bank and post office, they have no business operating your child's school.

Dr. Brad Hayton of the Pacific Policy Institute has said:

> America 2000 will cause more political conflict, the politicization of education, less cultural diversity, and more bureaucracy in the educational establishment. States and unions will become even more powerful, while teachers and parents will have less control of the content and practice of education.[12]

Many parents mistakenly think that America 2000 — often locally called Chicago 2000 or Baltimore 2000 depending on the city — is all about more parental involvement and power. It might start out that way, but, ultimately, any program funded by the federal purse will be controlled by the federal government itself. As a result, your voice will become so weak it won't even be heard.

Conservative activist, Phyllis Schlafly, quoted in the *Washington Post*, agrees, "Lip service is paid to local control, but the more we study the America 2000 prospectus, the more we conclude that locally elected school boards will become irrelevant because the federal money flow will drive the process."[13] How will they drive the process? By demanding strict adherence to their objectives. School boards who don't conform will pay the price.

Dr. Brad Hayton tells how this will happen:

> It rewards through money those who conform to its wishes, and it punishes others who do not conform by not funding or taxing. It also punishes those who do not conform by controlling employment standards, certification, college acceptance, and influencing accreditation. Thus schools and students who do not wish to conform to the national goals will not receive accreditation, funding, etc., and the students will find it increasingly difficult to pursue a college education or obtain employment.[14]

Your child's future will be determined by a few fat cats in Washington who have only one goal in mind: controlling the American people through bigger government. It's the old "big brother" theory reaching out to strangle individual initiative and community involvement.

The federal government has no business running education. Such power and control belong to parents, taxpayers, and elected local school board members.

Watizit?

The United States Department of Education has spent hundreds of thousands of dollars producing material to promote and explain America 2000. For the most part, the program is still very vague in its intent and objectives. This intended vagueness leaves it open for broad interpretation, thus making it potentially dangerous.

Robert Morrison, of the Family Research Council, who is editor of *Washington Watch* and a former Department of Education employee, told me recently that he thought the mascot for America 2000 should be borrowed from the 1996 Olympic mascot "Watizit." The odd shape of this mascot and the uncertainty of the creature's identity — described as a rain drop or even a sperm — gave rise to the name, "Watizit."

Once America 2000 takes to the field, American teachers, parents, and school boards will turn to one another in confusion and ask, "What is it?"

2

Goals 2000: Clinton's Baby

If America 2000 is so potentially dangerous, why was the Bush administration pushing this program? Because, when running for office, then Vice President George Bush stated he would become "the education president." Once he assumed office, Bush needed a program, and the National Governors Association was more than eager to hand him theirs.

Who was involved in the National Governors Association? Then Arkansas Governor Bill Clinton, along with former Secretary of Education Lamar Alexandria, and the current secretary, Bill Riley. While southern governors, these three men were members of the National Governors Association and the major architects of what is now known as America 2000.

In the beginning, America 2000 had something for everyone. This program offered school choice and merit pay for teachers to attract conservative legislators. For the liberals and unions, it provided increased nationalization as well as flexibility and increased funding for teachers. These added incentives were created to give President Bush political clout for re-election.

Obviously, it did not work.

Now, the Clinton administration has the power. You'd think any program promoted by a past Republican president should be nixed in the new liberal White House, right? Wrong! America 2000 is alive, well, and gaining momentum.

Of course, changes have been made. America 2000 is now called Goals 2000, and the program is more dangerous than ever.

The Governor's School

Jeoffrey Botkin in his factual documentary video, *The Guiding Hand: The Clinton Influence on Arkansas Education,* interviews former students, parents, and staff members who were involved with Bill Clinton's Governor's School in Arkansas. This six-week summer program, founded in 1979, was touted as a model for educational reform.

One former student, Steve Roberts, reveals the hidden agenda behind this prestigious school:

> They're taking the best, the cream of the crop . . . the leaders in our next generation and pushing into them the values that Governor Clinton has — that the leftist media has — the values that go totally against what this nation was founded on. This is what I was exposed to. There wasn't any warning, there wasn't anyone that said, "Okay, now you're going to have to take all the values that you grew up with and put them on the shelf and be exposed to this." If my parents had known what was going on there, they wouldn't have let me go.[1]

Shelvia Cole, a psychologist and concerned mother, describes how the students were isolated from their families and their values: "For those six weeks . . . they are not allowed to go home except for July the Fourth. They are discouraged from calling home and talking on the phone. They can receive mail, but they are encouraged to have as little contact with the outside world as possible. So it's a closed campus."[2]

Killi Wood, a former student, explains what one guest speaker told them: "Students, do me a favor. Totally ignore your parents. Listen to them, but then forget them. Because you need to start using your own stuff."[3]

In an effort to tear down the students' authority figure system, instructors try to convince the students that "You are the elite."

Mark Lowery, former director for Governor's School publicity, has now come out against the program. He says that students are told by instructors: "The reason why you're not going to be understood when you go home — not your parents, your friends, your pastor, or anybody — is because you have been treated to thoughts that they can't handle."[4]

The purpose of such propaganda is to develop an intellectual and cultural elitism that gives kids the right to say, "We know better than you."

In the video, Mark Lowery states:

> I think the whole intent of the governor's school in taking 350 - 400 students per summer, is to pick out the four, five, or six students that could be political leaders and then to mold their minds in this more liberal and humanistic thinking. . . . The greatest influence of the Governor's School is to promote the thought . . . that to be considered intellectual by your peers . . . you have to be a liberal thinker. . . . [This is] not teaching . . . but indoctrination.[5]

How was this indoctrination fostered? Liberal, anti-Christian values were promoted by forcing the students to watch pornographic movies about the gay lifestyle. I will refrain from describing some of the vile, filthy films these kids were exposed to during this six week period. Remember, this was a taxpayer funded program aimed at brainwashing the best and brightest students in Arkansas.

To get the full grasp of the radical mishmash that then Governor Clinton called this "exciting and unusual . . . educational adventure," you need to obtain a copy of Jeoffrey Botkin's documentary video, *The Guiding Hand: The Clinton Influence on Arkansas Education.* (See Resources section at end of this book.)

A New Age President?

After Clinton lost the governorship, his successor, Frank White, reviewed the Governor's School curriculum and called it "garbage." When Governor White tried to introduce more conventional moral values to the Governor's school, Clinton accused Governor White of "badgering educators."[6]

In the video exposing the Governor's School, Jeoffrey Botkin notes what happened as a result of Governor White's detective work. "The school simply went underground with its controversial philosophy until Clinton returned as governor. Since then the full curriculum at the Governor's School — including illegal psychological testing — has been more carefully concealed from parents and voters."[7]

In a documentary video promoting his school, Governor Bill Clinton enthusiastically endorsed his Governor's School: "It would be impossible for me to describe to you just how exciting and unusual this educational adventure is." The term, "unusual," certainly applies since the same video shows a group of students lying on the floor while a teacher asks, "Are you ready to divorce yourselves from your bodies?"

Sounds like New Age doctrine to me. Could it be that Bill Clinton accepts and promotes New Age thinking or is he just on a power trip? Maybe it's a little of both.

Michael Kelly in a *New York Times* article titled, "The New Year at a New Age Retreat," describes how Richard W. Riley, a champion for education reform and the president's educational secretary introduced the Clintons to a high-powered, New Age "Renaissance Weekend" retreat. According to Kelly, these "believers in Renaissance are hopeful that the spirit of rationalism will move the masses toward betterment."[8]

How best to influence the masses than by capturing the minds of the best and brightest among them?

Dr. Thomas Sowell in a *Forbes* magazine article, "Revelations for the Anointed," shows how the major social revolutions of the twentieth century were fueled by an intelligentsia with power to persuade the masses and seize their imagination. According to Sowell, those intent on fostering their "new" social philosophy considered logic and practical evidence to be insignificant to their goals. The intelligentsia believed that most people were content to follow a dream "without the drudgery of having to know the facts or cope with the complexities of life."[9]

In other words, "We'll tell you what to do. We know what's best for you simple-minded folks. Just follow our lead like a puppy with a new-found master."

Is that what we want for our children? Absolutely not!

A National School Board?

The same Bill Clinton, who was the foremost promoter of the mind-controlling Governor's School in Arkansas, now wants to take his New Age thinking into the classrooms of America. Remember that Bill Clinton, as governor of that state, "played a leading role in forging the six national goals for the year 2000."[10]

Senator Ted Kennedy and Senator Pell on April 29, 1993, proposed, through Senate Bill 846, a new federal agency to accomplish President Clinton's educational reforms. Pages 53-54 of the Senate version, reveals that these national goals will supersede state and local education requirements. Big federal dollars will be provided, and the goals will have to be met.[11]

Called Goals 2000: Educate America Act, it provides for establishing a National Goals Panel, a National Education Standards and Improvement Council, and a National Skill Standards Board, which will actually function like a national school board. Many of the twenty members would, of course, be hand picked by President Clinton.

Diane Ravitch, an assistant secretary of education in the Bush Administration, notes:

> All twenty members would be appointed by President Clinton, with no requirement for bipartisanship. By law, at least fifteen of the members would be professional educators, thus abandoning the tradition of lay control of education.[12]

That means they will undoubtedly be National Education Association (NEA) union members, not parents. All we need is a bunch of educational elitists and Washington bureaucrats telling our local school boards and school districts how and what to teach our children.

Some school boards and district administrators may think, "If we don't like the new reforms, we won't institute them in our schools." Remember, however, these are "National" Goals, "National" Standards, and a "National" Board. Sounds all inclusive to me.

Although the Clinton Administration's school reform bill describes participation in their "opportunities to learn" standards as "voluntary," that option will soon be blown away. Some members of Congress plan "to make these standards mandatory or to require them as a condition for federal financing."[13]

As always, money talks. But this time it may not be worth the price. According to Diane Ravitch:

> The Clinton Administration's new bill seems likely to add a new layer of bureaucracy, to impose reform from the top down and to dampen the innovative spirit that is now alive in thousands of schools and districts.[14]

What kind of people do you think President Clinton would select to fill these twenty prestigious and influential positions? We have only to look at a sampling of his recent cabinet and administrative appointments to get an idea.

Gays Get Special Treatment

According to the *Washington Watch* newsletter, the Clinton Administration "openly rejects qualified applicants for top federal positions because of race and gender." Homosexual applicants, however, are "assured of special treatment by the openly gay deputy director of presidential personnel, Bob Hattoy."[15]

The *Washington Watch,* provides these startling facts:

> President Clinton has named to top positions in his administration two officials who have tried to destroy the Boy Scouts of America. Lesbian radical Roberta Achtenberg of San Francisco and San Diego schools chief Thomas Payzant have used their power to expel the Scouts from public schools because the B.S.A. refuses to admit homosexuals or allow them to guide young boys.[16]

Payzant was named Clinton's assistant secretary for elementary and secondary education, and Achtenberg serves as under secretary of HUD! It scares me even to think what their agenda will be in these top level government positions. Why am I so worried?

The Platform/Action Statement for the April 25 Gay March on Washington, helps answer that question. Gay demands include "repeal of laws prohibiting sodomy;" provide "information on abortion, AIDS/HIV, child care, and sexuality courses at all levels of education;" end "discrimination based on sexual orientation in all programs of the Boy Scouts of America."[17]

In addition, the statement calls for an end to "discrimination against youth." What does that mean? They want to lower age-of-consent laws for sex with children! They also seek legalization to legalize same-sex marriages and adoption of children by gay couples.

Remember that Thomas Payzant was named Clinton's assistant secretary for elementary and secondary education. "So what?" you may ask. What's so terrible about a few homosexuals in high places? Once you read the plans they have for your children, you won't have to wonder any longer:

> "We shall sodomize your sons . . . we shall seduce them in your schools, in your dormitories, in your gymnasiums, in your locker rooms, in your sports arenas, in your seminaries, in your youth groups, in your movie theater bathrooms, in your army bunkhouses, in your truck stops, in your all-male clubs, in your houses of Congress, wherever men are with men together . . . . They will come to crave and adore us."
>
> "The family unit . . . will be abolished. The family unit, which only dampens imagination and curbs free will, must be eliminated."
>
> "All churches who condemn us will be closed. Our only gods are handsome young men . . . ."[18]

Don't fool yourself. Many homosexuals seek political power for only one reason: So they can push and lobby for their radical and dangerous proposals to the max.

Far from the Mainstream

The most telling of President Clinton's appointments is Jocelyn Elders for surgeon general. To expose her radical ideas, we have only to read the words spoken from her own mouth.

On CNBC's "Talk Live," Elders' startling opinion on drug abuse, prostitution, and birth control became clear in these few words: "I would hope that we would provide them [drug-abusing prostitutes] Norplant, so they could still use sex if they must to buy their drugs."

As for children and birth control, she said, "I don't know any parent who wouldn't go out at midnight and try to find contraceptives to start their children properly."[19]

Elders' view on sex education sounds another alarm: "We have driver's ed for our kids. We've taught them what to do in the front seat of the car, but not what to do in the back seat."[20]

And where would she like to start sex education? With five year olds! According to Elders, "An integral part of a comprehensive school-based health clinic today is that we have sexuality education beginning in kindergarten."[21] Under Elders' leadership as surgeon general, these school-based clinics would distribute condoms to students beginning in fifth grade.

Aside from Ms. Elders' radical ideas, President Clinton overlooked the fact that her past record suggests failure not success with these kinds of programs. An article in the *Washington Times,* notes, "Since Elders became Arkansas' health director in 1987, the teen pregnancy rate has risen 15 percent."[22] In addition, after two years of Jocelyn Elders, the teenage birthrate in Arkansas jumped from fourth highest in the U.S. in 1986 to the second highest in the U.S. in 1989.[23]

To make matters worse, between 1990 and 1992, syphilis rates in Arkansas skyrocketed while the U.S. rates declined. By 1992, the Arkansas syphilis rate was 92.3 per 100,000 population, while the U.S. rate was 45.3 per 100,000. To top it all, under Elders' leadership from 1989 to 1992, the number of cases of teenagers infected with HIV rose 150 percent.[24]

Once parents and teachers have followed Edlers' advice and taught kids what to do in the back seat and if the condoms supplied by the schools fail to do the job, what then? Elders provides the obvious alternative to teen pregnancy — abortion. She supports Medicaid funding for abortions[25] and plans to campaign to make the dangerous abortion drug, RU-486, available in the United States.[26]

In testimony before the Senate Labor Committee, in May 1990, Ms. Elders explains rather bluntly how she feels about abortion and its "positive" effect on society:

> Abortion has reduced the number of chil-
> dren afflicted with severe defects; the number of
> Down's Syndrome infants in Washington State in
> 1976 was 64 percent lower than it would have
> been without legal abortion.[27]

Now there's something we Americans can be proud of!
But don't disagree with Ms. Elders or you'll be labeled a
fanatic with "slave master" mentality. Here's her advice to
those of us who oppose the slaughter of unborn children: ". . .
really get over [your] love affair with the fetus."[28]

These statements paint a rather ominous picture of the
woman who controls the surgeon general's office and mandates our government's policies on health issues, abortion, and
substance abuse. If President Clinton can select someone so far
out of the mainstream of American life to this high office,
imagine what kind of people he'll pick for his national school
board.

The Clinton Mindset

Abraham Lincoln said, "The philosophy of education in
one generation will be the philosophy of government in the
next."[29] Unfortunately, the children of the last generation are in
the seats of power today.

A product of the 1960s, Bill Clinton, an admitted drug
user (but he didn't inhale), activist, draft dodger, and partici-
pant in the sixties peace movement, reflects the liberal mindset
of his generation. We have only to look back over the first
months of his presidency to see where Bill Clinton's sixties
education has brought us.

The *Washington Watch* newsletter, notes a few of the
dramatic social changes forced on the American people by Bill
Clinton and his liberal advisors within his first one hundred
days in office:

• *Recruiting homosexuals for the military.* Against the advice of Gen. Colin Powell, Gen. H. Norman Schwarkopf, the Joint Chiefs of Staff, the American Legion, the Veterans of Foreign Wars, 84 percent of retired officers and 74 percent of active duty enlisted volunteers, President Clinton seems determined to press homosexuals on the armed forces. He welcomed to the Oval Office gay leaders who demand that same-sex marriages be recognized by the military.

• *Taxing couples who marry.* . . . the Clinton Plan dredges up the "marriage penalty" which had been corrected by the 1986 Tax Reform Act. Under the Clinton plan, two young lovers making $140,000 each would save $5,425 in federal taxes by cohabiting instead of getting married.

• *Compelling abortion payments.* Despite opposition from 72 percent of Americans polled, President Clinton will force taxpayers to subsidize abortions in the military hospitals, domestic and international family planning, and government workers' insurance plans. He will also send taxpayers the bill for medical experiments using aborted children's organs.

• *Demanding admission of HIV+ immigrants.* President Clinton sought to lift the ban on admitting immigrants with AIDS. The House and the Senate rejected his proposals. Because Congress refused to spend an estimated $102,000 for each HIV+ immigrant, Clinton has bowed to the gay lobby by dropping his support for the entire spending bill for the National Institutes of Health.

• *Hampering the fight against crime.* President Clinton's attorney general, Janet Reno, fired all ninety-three U.S. attorneys. The move slowed active investigations into political corruption and will delay prosecution of child pornographers and obscenity violators.[30]

Still on Clinton's agenda is the lifting of the ban on the French RU-486 morning-after abortion bill.

Clinton's appointment of Donna Shalala as secretary for Health and Human Services provides more evidence of his liberal leanings. According to an article in the *Washington Post*, while Shalala was chancellor of the University of Wisconsin School of Medicine, "the Board of Regents implemented a written policy requiring politically correct speech. The document was so extreme it was declared unconstitutional by a federal court."[31]

The philosophy of today's educational system will surely continue to produce more leaders in government like Bill Clinton and his administrative appointments — unless the philosophy and purpose of education is drastically changed. Unfortunately, many of today's teachers and educators are also products of the sixties movement and have gained tenure in the educational system simply by spending time in the classroom. Their jobs are secure until retirement, and, as members of the National Education Association (NEA), they now have a friend in the White House.

3

School Choice: Why We Need It Now!

The only favorable part of America 2000 under the Bush Administration was the promotion of parental choice. The Clinton Administration scraped that option. Why? One reason could be that Secretary Richard W. Riley, a former two-term governor of South Carolina who orchestrated a sales tax increase in 1984 to fund changes in his state's school system, adamantly opposes school choice.

Within the first one hundred days of his administration, President Clinton opposed legislation to help parents choose their children's schools. Although Bill and Hillary had the option of selecting a private religious school for their daughter, they do not want you to have the same freedom.

The Clinton Administration also opposes the voucher system. Such a program would make it possible for many parents who currently cannot afford a private school education to be able to do so. The program would allow parents to receive a voucher in the amount that they already spend through taxes to the local public school. This voucher could then be credited toward the tuition at a private school. The private school would then simply send the voucher to the state, redeem it for its cash value, and put the money toward the child's tuition.

Why would President Clinton and liberal politicians fight against a policy that would strengthen public schools and provide for better student education? Rush Limbaugh provides the answer to this question:

> The average family pays thousands of dollars a year into the public school system. Parents should be able to take that money and spend it on a school — public or private — that teaches the values they believe are important for their kids. Moreover, it has been argued that the reason why liberals are so adamant about busing and forced integration, and against choice in secondary education, is that the public schools are the only remaining grounds for liberal ideas. It's where new little liberals are shaped and formed amid an avalanche of liberal propaganda that has made its way into the curriculum.[1]

Aside from the liberals in Washington, another powerful force is lobbying to keep parents from having a say in their child's education. In fact, school choice and the voucher system may be killed. Why? Because of the political pressure and influence the National Education Association and other teachers unions have on the Clinton administration.

During the presidential campaign, Bill Clinton, in acknowledging the support of the NEA — the largest union in the United States — said, "If I become president, you'll be my partners. I won't forget who brought me to the White House."

The NEA's Power Goals

What does the NEA want from President Clinton? Let's look at a few of their "power goals" as documented in *Forbes* magazine's June 7, 1993, cover story, "The National Extortion Association."

The NEA demands "early childhood education programs in the public schools for children from birth through age eight."[2] Phyllis Schlafly, in commenting on this "demand," writes:

> Since the public schools have done such a poor job of educating kids from age six to eighteen, who but the NEA could, with a straight face, think it would be a good idea to turn over infants and toddlers to them, too?[3]

And what does the NEA plan to do once they get your kids enrolled in their "education programs"? Here's a clue. The NEA demands that "guidance and counseling programs should be integrated into the entire education system, beginning at the pre-kindergarten level."[4] Apparently, these educators think young children need, in Phyllis Schlafly's words: "group psychotherapy at every grade level, regardless of parental wishes."[5]

The NEA goes on to assert "the right of every individual (i.e., school children of any age) to live in an environment of freely available information, knowledge, and wisdom about sexuality."[6] In other words, "Parents, butt out; the schools are going to tell primary school children all about how to engage in sex and with what devices."[7]

In addition, the NEA demands that every student have "immediate, direct, and confidential access to health, social, and psychological services."[8] What does that mean? According to Phyllis Schlafly, "confidential" means "without parents being informed when their children are given contraceptives and other sex services"[9] — including abortion counseling.

After reading the *NEA Handbook,* their political agenda becomes apparent:

> • The NEA strongly supports the hiring of homosexual teachers. In fact, the NEA views homosexuality as an acceptable lifestyle.

- The NEA believes that union contracts with local school boards should require all teachers to pay dues or fees to the union.
- The NEA is opposed to merit pay for teachers.
- The NEA is opposed to voluntary prayer in schools.
- The NEA opposes tuition tax credit legislation.
- The NEA is opposed to the use of school facilities after school for voluntary religious meetings.
- At the last two Democratic National Conventions, over 20 percent of the delegates were NEA members.
- The NEA favors increased federal funding and NEA control of primary and secondary education.
- The NEA advocates putting school-based clinics, with contraceptive services and abortion referrals, in our public schools.
- The NEA is in favor of forced busing of school children to achieve a "racial balance."[10]

Why is an organization that is so out of touch with mainstream America permitted to determine the educational policies for the nation's children? At the same time, they use their political clout to make sure they maintain their control of the educational system overall.

NEA v. California Parents

Some states, however, are fighting back.

In November Californians will vote on Proposition 174, which, if passed, would allow for school choice and the voucher system. Guess who's trying to defeat the California initiative? None other then the NEA (The National Education Association), which some call "The National Extortion Association."[11]

The NEA, at its annual convention in San Francisco in July 1993, contributed $1 million to defeat the school choice initiative on the California ballot. Keith Geiger, president of the NEA, "threw down the gauntlet against parents" and said, "There's no better cause for that money."[12]

That's only the beginning. California's NEA plans to spend $10 million to defeat the Nov. 2, 1993, initiative, and their state president, Del Weber, believes, "There are some proposals that are so evil that they should never be presented to the voters."[13]

What's so evil about letting parents decide where to send their kids to school, especially when it saves taxpayer dollars? According to Phyllis Schlafly, "Each school child whose parents exercise the choice would henceforth cost the taxpayers only $2500 per year (the price of the voucher) instead of $5000 (the price of keeping the child in public school.) But the NEA isn't about saving the taxpayer's money; it's about retaining control over the minds of school children."[14]

Getting Your Money's Worth

Wisconsin State Representative, Polly Williams, authored and promoted a bill allowing for a voucher system program in Milwaukee that currently has six hundred students enrolled. Because of her efforts, Ms. Williams is being hailed as a heroine in the fight for equality in education for the poor and low income.

On Sunday, August 29, 1993, Polly Williams made the following comment as a guest on NBC's "This Week with David Brinkley:"

> If you have money, position, and power you can have a good school for your child. But if you happen to be poor or low income, you don't have those choices and that's not right. All the opponents [of school choice] are talking about maintaining a system . . . that's not working. We are talking about saving our children. Parents should

have the right to take their children out of bad systems that are not addressing their needs. Taxpayer's dollars are being spent to maintain these systems that don't work. What is wrong with parents taking money and going to another school of their choice to help save their children?

Opponents claim that school choice and the voucher system is not fair because it only allows for the middle- and upper-income families to leave the schools. They call this "white flight" and suggest the poor and low income will be stuck sitting in the classrooms alone.

Stop and ask yourself: "Why are the middle- and upper-income families leaving the public schools for private education?" Because the schools are not doing the job, and these families are not getting their money's worth. Fortunately for them, they can afford to send their children to better schools, even if it means paying not only for a public education through taxes but also a private school tuition.

The liberals claim that conservatives want school choice in order to segregate both race and class. This is absolutely false. We are not interested in segregation, but education — real education for all of America's children. In reality, the liberals are the ones who want to prevent the less fortunate from prospering.

If the liberals were really interested in the poor and low income as they claim, they would be standing with Polly Williams, fighting for school choice and the voucher system. Then they — like the middle and upper class — would have the option to leave the bad schools behind instead of being left behind.

Cambridge, Massachusetts, has proved that choice works. Its twelve-year-old school choice program is considered to be one of the best in the country even though it is limited to public schools. Kathy Palarski, a parent of five had this to say about the public school her children attend in Cambridge: "That was considered one of the poorest schools in the city, but now it is one of the most requested. It is filled; you can't get in there."

How Much Worse Can It Get?

Why are the liberals who scream for economic equality in education standing in the way of the one program that will work — school choice? Because, as we already know, the liberals are more interested in propping up a failing system than in educating children.

Democratic Governor Roy Romer of Colorado, who helped defeat the school voucher system in his state last year, proves my point when he told David Brinkley: "I'll admit up front, if the system gets so bad, and it's really hurting people, you're going to have to give up and find another alternative. I don't think we are there yet. If we fail totally, then I admit we ought to give people choice."

Pray tell, why should we wait until the system totally fails before we do something? That's like saying, "I know my cholesterol level is too high, but I'm not going to do anything about it until I have a heart attack." That would be stupid, right?

Governor Romer said we need to wait until the system gets so bad that it's hurting people before we find an alternative. Has the governor been living under a rock? Already "three-fifths of the students in America's schools who reach their senior year of high school either don't graduate or graduate with less than seventh grade skills."[15] How much worse can we let the system get? Could it be that the liberal elite have a hidden motive behind their desire to keep America's youth trapped in a decaying system?

You see, if we end up with a system where everyone — regardless of income — can receive a top notch education, we might end up with people who are educated. If we end up with people who are educated, the liberals might find themselves out of jobs. Why? Because an educated populace would not be stupid enough to believe their lies. Not to mention that those who are educated can go on to get good jobs and make something of themselves, instead of being dependent on the liberal's social handouts.

Parents Know Best

Polly Williams has said that not allowing for school choice and the voucher system for the poor and low income is "an insult to parents." Why? Ms. Williams explains:

> It says that low-income families don't have the sense to know how to choose what is best. Only these bureaucrats and these educrats, and these professionals know what is best. You are insulting parents when you talk about the fact that they're going to pick a school that's not going to help their children. They're fighting now to get them out of public school because they're not helping their children!

Ms. Williams is no fool. She knows that parents know best.

Opponents of school choice, in trying to bolster their argument, like to throw out this question: Why should the American taxpayer have to pay for someone's child to go to a private school?

Well, first off, the money for the voucher is not coming out of anyone's pocket except that of the parent who is receiving the voucher. That's not to mention the fact most states only allow about a third of the money paid into the system through taxes to be used as a voucher for a private school. This means two-thirds of the tax money is automatically given to the public school in the district where the student resides even though the student doesn't attend the public school.

It seems to me the question that should be asked is: Why should the parents of students paying tuition for private education have to continue to support a failing public school system with their hard-earned tax dollars?

I leave you with the words of the "Moses" of school choice and the voucher system, Bill Bennett: "If the people in that community like that school and want to maintain it, let them stay. If they don't, let the people go. This is the United States of America."[16]

Power to the Parents!

Michigan's governor, John Engler, is taking a different approach. In an attempt "to wrest control of public education from the mostly liberal education lobby," he hopes to return power to parents, whom he thinks "should make decisions about the basic curriculum, elective courses, education goals — even the schools in which they want their children to be educated."[17]

Governor Engler pushed a bill through the state legislature that reduces property taxes that are paid by home owners to fund local school districts. Syndicated columnist Cal Thomas explains the reason for this unusual action: "Because there is a legislative prohibition against using state funds to aid private schools, Engler wants to devise a state 'scholarship' program that will allow parents to choose the schools their children attend, including private religious schools." In addition, the governor believes "teachers will even be able to create their own schools."[18]

This revolutionary idea is diametrically opposed to plans proposed by President Clinton and congressional Democrats. The only way they know to bring about "change" is to raise more taxes to build more bureaucracy and gain more control over the people. In contrast, "Governor Engler is not only returning money and power to people but also a sense of mastery over their own destinies."[19]

For example, studies show that parochial schools save taxpayers billions of dollars. Why? Because "they are cost-effective, quality institutions whose existence is a benefit to everyone, including public schools."[20] No wonder, especially when the New York City public school system employs 32,000 school administrators, which is about 12,000 more administrators than all the schools in Europe!

In fact, Mayor David Dinkins of New York City referred

to Catholic schools as the "single most important non-profit partner in balancing the city's books." If these schools closed, it would cost the Big Apple $220 million.[21]

In addition, the education advantages are far superior. New York City's public schools have a 25 percent dropout rate while the seventy-nine inner city Catholic schools serve 31,000 students and have a less than 1 percent dropout rate. In fact, although 90 percent of parochial students come from families at or below the federal poverty level, nine out of ten graduates go on to higher education.[22] That's a remarkable achievement for any school system!

Scared Out of Their Wits

Academic achievement is only one reason why parents deserve a choice in where to send their kids. Charles Glenn, a prominent educator and researcher, writes that "diversity of schooling is necessary in education because it permits a better match of the individual child with the appropriate educational setting."[23]

What is an appropriate educational setting? Most of us would agree it is a safe environment that fosters learning without fear of violence. For many kids who attend public schools, that definition is only a dream. In a recent *USA Weekend* magazine poll of 65,000 teens, 39 percent responded that they did not feel safe at their public school, and 50 percent knew someone who had switched to a safer school environment.[24]

Why are kids worried about their safety? Because "one in twenty students carries a gun to school, and seventy-one killings have taken place in our schools in the last four years.[25] In addition, 55 percent of tenth-twelfth graders polled said they knew somebody who carried a weapon to school."[26]

Leslie Ansley, in her article for *USA Weekend,* "It Just Keeps Getting Worse," reports that "each hour, 2,000 U.S. students are physically attacked on school grounds; each day, more than 160,000 students skip school out of fear." To bring the point home, Ansley provides these examples:

An Antioch, California, high school boy burst into a classroom, stabbed a girl, and tried to set her on fire. No clear motive was discovered. . .. In a Harlem, Georgia, school corridor, a ninth-grader shot another boy to death and hurt a second student. . . . A Dartmouth, Massachusetts, ninth-grade boy was stabbed to death in a classroom by three boys looking for a fight."[27]

What do most students want? Is a safe educational environment too much to ask? Sixty-three percent say they would learn more if they felt safer, and most would be happier in general if they didn't have to worry about their safety at school. Children deserve the right to attend a school that will protect them physically and educate them properly.

The Educational Monopoly

Would you shop at a mall that allowed gang members to roam the halls and threaten other shoppers? I don't think so. Why not? Because you could choose to shop somewhere else. Eventually the owners of the unsafe mall would either take measures to protect their customers or go out of business. That's the way our free enterprise system works.

Presently, however, America's educational system does not operate in an open market — it functions as a monopoly. Parents and students, in many cases, have no other choice than their local public school.

What would it take to create a more competitive and quality educational system? Former U.S. Congressman Jack Kemp, who later served as HUD secretary under the Bush Administration, provides the answer to that question:

Give parents access to private as well as public schools. When parents are involved in choosing where to send their precious children, they take a greater interest. Where principals are more accountable to parents and to the quality of

the education that the children are going to receive, they become more responsible for hiring
and firing teachers who do not teach. We need
more competition for the public school, and it can
only come from private schools, be they Jewish,
Catholic, evangelical, private, or secular.[28]

Robert Morrison of the Family Research Council in an
article titled, "Americans Choosing Schools," stresses how
school choice increases competition and, ultimately, improvement all around:

All parents, regardless of income, should be
able to choose places where they know their
children will learn. And they should be able to
choose environments where their own values will
be extended instead of lost. It's possible that there
are some public schools nobody would choose.
They are so bad they might find themselves without any students. But I have no idea why we
should be interested in protecting schools like that
from competition — or any schools from competition. Our worst schools are our non-competitive
ones, and that's no coincidence. We need to break
the monopoly currently exercised by state-run
schools and allow all schools — including private
and religious schools — to compete for public
dollars. A full-scale voucher program would promote a healthy rivalry between public and private
schools, as well as among public schools.[29]

Almost every other monopoly in our society's history
has failed. In light of that fact, Pat Robertson on CBN's "700
Club" offered this hopeful perspective concerning the public
school educational monopoly: "It's going to fall apart and be
replaced by something better."

Let's hold on to that word of encouragement while we

fight to protect our children from being shot in their classrooms or mentally abducted by the educational elite.

Forcing Private Schools to Conform

The fight, however, will be an uphill battle. Why? Because once Clinton's Goals 2000 is in place, even Christian schools will be forced to conform to the national curriculum and national testing. Those who refuse will be subject to excessive taxation and/or lose their certification credentials until they comply.

Already, the long arm of the government is trying to control the private school sector as much as possible. In South Dakota, all students in both private and public schools, as well as home schoolers, must be given standardized tests in fourth, eighth, and eleventh grades. Recently, however, the state has mandated that only the Stanford Achievement Test be used. Many Christian school officials do not object to giving standardized tests, but they don't like being told which test to administer.

Although the Stanford test is currently given in many Christian schools, teachers have noticed that certain questions reflect a humanistic and relativistic trend. As a result, some Christian schools prefer standardized tests that measure academic knowledge and not the attitudes or personal preferences of students. In order to have their students pass these more subjective sections of the Stanford tests, Christian school teachers would either have to teach their children the politically correct answers or let them fail these sections.

As it stands now, the national results of the Stanford Achievement Test are published every year. Private school test scores, however, are not included in the statistics. Why? Could it be because private school students overall score much higher, and the comparison would reflect poorly on the public schools?

The Association of Christian Schools International, with which many private Christian schools are affiliated, provides convincing statistics on their higher quality of educational achievement. Year after year, testing shows that ACSI students score at or above the national average at every grade level on the Stanford Achievement Test (SAT). In fact, in grades one through four, Christian school students are consistently five to nine months ahead of their public school counterparts.[30] This trend could be broken if tests begin to focus more on attitudes rather than academics, putting Christian students at a distinct disadvantage.

The "Politically Correct" SAT

The problem of subjective testing will also affect college bound students. Revisions are currently being made to the Scholastic Aptitude Test (SAT), which generally determines student acceptance into about 2,000 colleges and universities. The new version, the biggest overhaul of the SAT in nearly fifty years, will be released by the national College Board in the spring of 1994. How is the test being changed?

John Katzman, president of the Princeton Review, one of the nation's largest providers of SAT prep courses says, "The test is PC (politically correct)." Although the new test reflects a shift toward critical reading and away from the multiple-choice format that has dominated the SAT, Katzman notes that "the key to reading questions isn't the reading — it's the questions."[31] In other words, comprehending the material presented is not nearly as important as figuring out what the politically correct answer or attitude should be.

In addition, the method of calculating final test results has been changed in favor of the students. According to the *Index of Leading Cultural Indicators,* the same person taking the same SAT test and putting down the same answers would score between 18 and 39 points higher in 1992 than in 1960.[32] In spite of that advantage, "SAT scores have dropped nearly 80 points in the past three decades while spending has increased significantly."[33] In fact, in the last decade, per pupil spending has risen 90.3 percent — more than twice the rate of inflation.[34]

A federal report released to Americans September 8, 1993, revealed that there are forty million American's who are

illiterate, and fifty million who are "barely making the grade."
My friends, we are spending more on education than national
defense and this report proves that we are not getting our
money's worth. Another question I have is, How could these
people graduate unable to read? This says a lot about our
educational system.

Now — Before It's Too Late

We need school choice now. Why? Because after the
educational elite "fix" the educational system, what will we
have to choose from?

One of the demands of the National Education Association (NEA), is "mandatory kindergarten and heavy regulation
of home-schooling, with curriculum approved in advance by
an NEA-staffed agency."[35]

Isn't that why many parents have opted out of public
education and dedicate themselves to the task of home-schooling in the first place? So they can control the kind of material
their children are taught?

The NEA, however, can't stand the fact that thousands of
parents have chosen to teach their children at home. Their
elitist mindset finds it inconceivable that "untrained" parents
could possibly implement the mechanics of teaching. As a
result, they look with disdain on anyone who will not submit
to their NEA "standards."

Dr. Brad Hayton of the Pacific Policy Institute notes the
danger behind such thinking:

> If the national government prescribed the
> size, contents, price, etc. of all hamburgers made
> in America, while subsidizing fast food chains
> that adhered to their standards, it would be readily
> apparent that they were not for more diversity in
> consumer choice. One must have something to
> choose from. If everything is the same, then there
> is no choice.[36]

William Bennett, former secretary of education in the Bush Administration, adds this analogy: "Today there are greater, more certain, and more immediate penalties in this country for serving a single rotten hamburger than for furnishing a thousand school children with a rotten education."[37]

Some educationalists see the handwriting on the wall, however, and are making use of every available opportunity to put the competition — the private schools — out of business. In South Dakota, the State Department of Education sent a letter to every state congressman and state senator advising them not to consider the private school sector when determining requirements for school certification. As a result, the requirements could be financially impossible for the Christian schools to meet, forcing them to close.

Why do many liberals and the educational elite desire to see the private school sector go under? Because they want to eliminate any threat to their public school breeding ground for liberalism, atheism, relativism, and political correctness.

Why are some politicians and educationalists running scared? Because polls show that 70 percent of the American people want an alternative to the public schools since they are not providing their children with quality education. In addition, "almost half of all urban public school teachers with school-age children send their children to private schools"[38] and 22 percent of public school teachers overall choose private education for their kids. That really makes you wonder, doesn't it?

Suppose there were a great outcry by the American people against governmental control of education? What would the educational elite do? They could offer school choice to silence the public in an effort to convince parents they had won the battle. But what good is school choice, once the government has control with President Clinton's Goals 2000 and all the schools are the same? What will we have to choose from?

4

Robbing the Cradle: Parents as Teachers

Parents as teachers. Sounds like a good idea. But is it?

Laura Rogers, former researcher with the Moore Foundation, has grave doubts and says the "Parents as Teachers" educational program that has been introduced in at least forty states and eight countries, " . . . will result in state control of the children and reduce parents to the status of breeders and supervised custodians."[1]

Laura Rogers, a mother of six and founder of the St. Charles Christian School in St. Charles, Missouri, which she has operated for twenty years, ought to know. As a lobbyist for the Missouri home school law — which has been used as a model nationally — Laura has appeared on the "Today Show," "Point of View," and other programs discussing her Christian school and research related to home schooling and the "Parents as Teachers" program.

Goal Number One of the six national goals of America 2000 allows for the implementation of early childhood intervention programs such as "Parents as Teachers" and states:

"All children will start school ready to learn." Although this sounds valid, it is a smoke screen hiding the true mission of America 2000.

According to Phyllis Schlafly, president and founder of the pro-family group, Eagle Forum, "The first goal of America 2000 to deal with children before they enter school is extremely ominous." She particularly finds the Parents as Teachers Program "extremely objectionable."[2]

Why? Because, as Mrs. Schlafly points out, "Parents as Teachers should be called Teachers as Parents. Schools are trying to substitute as parents and take over the raising of the children from infancy — something the government and the schools have no competence to do."[3]

On page 29, of the America 2000 legislation, the statement is made:

> Increased attention will be focused on adult behavior, responsibility for children and family, and community values essential for strong schools. This includes involving parents as teachers of their children and as school partners.[4]

Implemented by Missouri in 1981, this program was supposed to help avert a rising drop-out rate and increase parental support of the educational system. In 1985, the Missouri legislature passed a resolution "offering" — which means requiring — all 543 school districts in Missouri the Parents as Teachers program.

Based on a study conducted by nationally renowned child development expert, Dr. Burton White, who served as a consultant to the four pilot projects launched in 1981, this program does not encourage parents to be teachers of their children. The real purpose is to teach *parents* how to parent according to the standards set by the program.

Get 'Em Early

Legislation to provide funding for "early intervention"

programs such as "Parents as Teachers" was introduced as U.S. Senate Bill 1134, on May 22, 1991, and later tabled. It is still waiting to be reintroduced.

Although at this time "Parents as Teachers" is not a national program, it has been implemented in many states by their departments of education. Introduced on January 11, 1991, the pending Congressional Bill called, H.R. 520, would make "Parents as Teachers" a national program. It also has been temporarily tabled.

The bill states, "Most early childhood programs begin at age three or four when remediation may already be necessary."[5] Remediation from what? Three years of parental love, guidance, and supervision?

Although the program is currently voluntary, it could become mandatory if parents are not made aware of pending legislation and do not take the necessary action.

How does the program work? A family volunteers for what is presented as education and health screening to ensure that their child begins school healthy and ready to learn. If the child is not ready, the program also assures the parents that the school will help that child learn by meeting his or her individual needs.

Although presented as a voluntary program, once parents enlist, they have a hard time opting out without harassment from "parent educators." If parents refuse to stay in the program or do not follow their advisor's instructions, the advisor will threaten to contact local child protection services to have the child removed from the home. Several documented cases have shown that after a family has dropped out of the program, within a few days, a social worker shows up at the child's home!

Surely, that can't happen in America. Yet, I have talked to numerous creditable family advocates who have confirmed that such harassment definitely takes place.

Parents and Children At Risk

The House Bill defines the "parent educator" as "a person

hired by the lead agency of a state or designated by local entities who administers group meetings, home visits and developmental screening. . . ."[6] In order for the states to continue to receive federal grants for this program, there would have to be, "a minimum of four group meetings and eight home visits for each participating family."

Laura Rogers makes this observation:

> A "parent educator" bonds herself to a family through home visits or school visits in order to help parents feel more comfortable about leaving their child(ren) at the center. Both parents and children are evaluated under the guise of educational screening.[7]

In Missouri where "Parents as Teachers" (PAT) had its start, measures were taken to protect family confidentiality. Home educators are not permitted to share with anyone the information they collect during their visits. Yet, Missouri's open records law grants public access to any of the PAT documents. So much for confidentiality!

Laura Rogers makes another startling revelation about what the "parent educator" determines from her visit:

> The child is given a personal computer code number by which he can be tracked the rest of his life. There are twelve computer code definitions which label the child "at risk." Since the expectation is that every child will be found "mentally ill," there is no code for normal.[8]

Why would every pre-school child be considered mentally ill? Dr. Pierce, a promoter of America 2000, provides the answer,

> Every child in America who enters school at the age of five is mentally ill because he comes to

school with allegiance toward our elected officials, toward our founding fathers, toward our
institutions, toward the preservation of this form
of government, patriotism, nationalism, sover-
eignty . . . all of that proves the children are sick,
because the truly well individual is one who has
rejected all of those things and is what I would call
the true international child of the future.[9]

Does that give you a clue as to what these "educators"
have up their sleeve? They want to re-program your child's
mind and beliefs to their way of thinking.

How "Sick" is Your Child?

Who determines, then, how "sick" your child is? The
power to label your child "at risk" belongs to the friendly
"home educator" who visits your house regularly and makes
notes about every aspect of your family life.

What kind of training does a person in such a responsible
position receive? Only one week — a mere thirty hours — is
all that is required to make them "experts" on parenting and
evaluators of your child's future.

What criteria does the "home educator" use to assess
your child? These are the twelve "at risk" codes. See where
you, your child, and your family fit in:

- Premature babies, emergency delivery, or
birth trauma.
- A child's slow growth, poor appetite, or
frequent illness.
- Delayed development. (By whose definition is this measured?)
- Inability of parents to cope with inappro-
priate child behavior, including spanking as exclusive form of discipline, and inconsistency.
- A parent who is ill, heavy, tired, depressed,
handicapped, injured, or appears to be of low-
level intelligence.

    • Overindulgence, undue spoiling on part of parent.

    • Stress on the family, such as a parent that travels frequently, moving to a new home, a death in the family, divorce or separation, birth of a sibling, three children under the age of three, prolonged illness, loss of a job, low level income.

    • Allergies, heavy cigarette smoking in the house, family history of hearing loss, lack of stimulation or over stimulation, predominantly inappropriate or very few toys.[10]

If the Senate Bill 1133, which is called "Comprehensive Services for Children and Youth Act of 1991," ever passes and your family meets any of these characteristics, you could be classified as a "dysfunctional family." Thus you would be "at risk" all right — at risk of losing your child to the state, where they could be raised correctly, as the state sees fit!

Cradle to College

What is the real purpose of the "home educator"?

    Yale psychologist, Edward Zigler, calls home visitation programs run by government authorities, "an essential part of my vision of the school of the twenty-first century." That vision calls for parents to turn over primary care of infants to home-based day care providers (after taking a short-term post-birth job leave). These home day care providers would be linked to the public school system, which also would offer school-based day care for children aged three and four as well as before and after-school care for school aged children and a variety of other social services directed to children. Thus Zigler's school of the twenty-first century hopes largely to supplant the role of parents from "cradle to college."[11]

They want your children. It's as simple as that. Of course, they approach it under the guise of helping parents parent their children. But what kinds of families does the PAT program target?

> Were the PAT program targeted only to families with a proven track record of dysfunction (families of divorce, domestic violence, illegitimacy, etc.), then this "parental inadequacy assumption" might be justified. Given, however, that the program is intended to be a "preventative" program geared to ordinary families, this assumption is pernicious and has a counterproductive effect. Moreover, there is little research evidence to suggest that home visitation contributes meaningfully to positive development outcomes. In fact, a 1988 study of an experimental mother-child program found that home visitation did not improve parenting skill or child development.[12]

If home visitation doesn't work and the homes they target don't need help anyway, why are the educators pushing the PAT program? Remember, it's the first goal of America 2000. Here's an idea of what they have in mind.

Lamer Alexander, former secretary of education, in promoting America 2000, proclaimed that schools need to be open from six in the morning till six at night, supply children with all three meals, and provide the necessary social services. Mr. Alexander said he felt that even *babies* should be in school!

You can see that the educational elite are out of touch with reality and have lost all rational judgment when it comes to the true purpose and function of education. They consider schools factories where children — considered property of the state — are put on a classroom conveyer belt and molded into little liberal robots.

What would be the result of such a homeless climate? Recent history provides the answer:

Marxist states sought more control over childrearing via institutional day care and other policies that separated children from their parents and grandparents. We see today in the fouled environments of Eastern Europe and Russia, in the corrosive ethnic hatreds that boil below the surface of socialist fraternity, and in the rotting, outmoded industrial plants of the Eastern Bloc the fruits of a policy that ignored the rights of parents and that treated religious and moral beliefs as subversive of the state.[13]

"That could never happen in America," you say? Let's hope not, but many parents and educators are alarmed at the direction our government is taking.

Medication and Vaccinations

Do you have a hyper-active child? If so, read this section carefully.

There have been reports of "home educators" recommending that parents with supposedly hyper-active children see a doctor and receive a prescription for Ridalin — a potentially addictive drug. Parents who followed the home educator's instructions, but who later refused to give Ridalin to their children, were reported — by the "home educator" — to child protection services.

Katie Soffin, a researcher on "Parents as Teachers" and Outcome Based Education wanted to find out if such reports were true. As the director of "PAT Answers" and a staff writer with *Kansas City Christian Newspaper*, Mrs. Soffin conducted the following interview.

In November of 1991, I called the child abuse hotline to find out further details on how they handled reports and if they handled reports from parent educators. They told me they did.

> I asked if a "parent educator" were to recommend that a parent see a doctor to prescribe Ridalin, and the parent saw the doctor, was given a prescription, but refused to give Ridalin to their child, would the parent educator call the child abuse hotline? They replied, "Yes."
>
> "What happens with the report from there?" I asked.
>
> They replied, "The case is given to a social worker who then contacts the parent educator and the physician. The three of them decide whether or not to deliver an ultimatum to the parent to either give their child Ridalin or the child will be removed from the home."
>
> I could not believe what they told me.[14]

In Missouri and several states, parent educators or state agents are required by law to report individuals who do not comply with "recommended" services. Failure by a state employee to report noncompliance is a class A misdemeanor, punishable by one thousand dollars and/or one year in jail.

To make matters worse, the Clinton Administration has unveiled its aggressive strategy to track every child in the U.S. How do they plan to do that? By providing age-appropriate immunizations for every child. This goal of assuring vaccinations for all American children against childhood diseases, however, includes a questionable plan to register and track all children and families by their Social Security numbers.[15]

Many responsible parents are concerned that this bill will threaten family privacy. Meanwhile, Clinton sent a letter to those participating in the April 25 homosexual march on Washington lauding the group's aims, which include continuing anonymous and only voluntary HIV testing. Healthy children would be tracked by our government, but adults with a lethal, transmissible disease will remain anonymous.[16]

Health and Human Services secretary, Donna Shalala, told Congress that President Clinton plans to buy up *all* U.S.

vaccine production and dispense it "free" to *all* American children.[17]

That statement raises questions every parent should be asking: Does that mean the government will have a monopoly on all available vaccines? What will happen to those parents who refuse to participate in the government immunization program? Will they be considered child abusers? Will someone from child protection services show up at their house with a threat to comply or risk losing their children?

Such a scenario is not beyond our imagination in light of what has been happening in the Parents as Teachers program.

It's the Money!

In 1992, U.S. Senate Bill S.B. 1275 was introduced and tabled for that session. The bill was asking for $100 million for the "Parents as Teachers" National Center in St. Louis, Missouri, in order to promote their programs nationally. The bill was introduced by U.S. Senator Christopher Bond who was governor of Missouri when PAT was introduced.

> Parents as Teachers National Center includes 22 influential people, not the least of whom are: John Ashcroft, governor of Missouri (R); Christopher Bond, U.S. senator from Missouri (R); Richard Gephart, U.S. congressman from Missouri, House Majority Leader (D); and Ed Zigler, Yale University early childhood education specialist and social planner.[18]

Why is this program so popular with the states? Because they receive federal money for developing early childhood prevention programs. The more "at risk" children they have, the more money they receive. Governors are also told in the America 2000 legislation that they will receive national recognition and funding for implementing this early childhood intervention program.

If "Parents as Teachers" was geared toward helping

families with problems because of divorce, drugs, alcohol abuse, and or child abuse, I could see the legitimacy of such a program. But PAT is a voluntary program. What dysfunctional family would invite a home educator into their home to evaluate them?

Most of the families involved in this program are good parents who care about their children. Why else would they have volunteered for a program that was marketed as "health and educational screening" to prepare their child for school? Would an irresponsible parent enlist in such a program? Of course not!

The pushers of PAT know that, but their main goal is to get into homes and control how parents are raising their kids regardless of their needs or what kind of parents they find.

Where will the "Parents as Teachers" program eventually lead us? To the licensing of parents, as William B. Maxwell, an attorney from Oklahoma, has recommended. Parents may one day be forced to go through parenting training before receiving a marriage license or before being permitted to enroll a child in school.

What happens if you don't meet their criteria as a qualified parent? I think you know the answer.

The time to act is now. We cannot wait until America 2000 and "Parents as Teachers" becomes a nationally mandated program with the hidden agenda of abducting our children from the safety and security of their own homes.

5

Achieving Mediocrity: Outcome Based Education

The National Commission on Excellence in Education declared in 1983, that the United States was a nation at risk. The report stated:

> The educational foundations of our society are presently being eroded by a rising tide of mediocrity that threatens our very future as a nation and a people.[1]

Have our students improved since 1983? Let's look at some statistics.

In the 1992 International Test Comparison in science, American students ranked thirteenth, answering only 67 percent of the questions correctly. This score placed the U.S. behind countries such as Korea, Taiwan, the Soviet Union, Slovenia, Israel, Canada, and France.[2]

Other studies show that "fewer than one in seven students in grades four, eight, and twelve can do mathematics at or above their grade level. More than half are two or more grade levels behind."[3]

This is certainly not the time for the implementation of a program such as Outcome Based Education that has no proven track record of success. W.R. Daggett, author of *Preparing Students for the 1990s and Beyond,* tells us why:

> The skills necessary for the work place are changing at a rate four to five times faster than curriculum and organizational structure in schools, leaving a gap between what students learn and what will be expected of them in the work place.[4]

Outcome Based Education (or OBE) will only widen this gap and give rise to an ever increasing acceptance in mediocrity. In addition, it will flood our nation with uneducated, unqualified adults who will be attempting to enter the workplace. What will be the result? Skyrocketing unemployment and underemployment.

A New Credo

Many parents across the country have banned together to oppose this educational reform program known as Outcome Based Education. Why the opposition? Most dislike governmental invasion into parental territory through the teaching and testing of attitudes and values and the modification of their child's behavior.

Lily Wong Filmore, professor of language at the University of California at Berkeley, explains OBE's agenda: "No matter what their parents and families think about others or the environment . . . we are going to have to inculcate in our children the rules that form a credo that will work for a multicultural twenty-first century.[5]

Developed by Theodore Sizer, William Spady, and William Glasser, Outcome Based Education has many names and is referred to as Mastery Learning, Restructuring, Relearning, or Cooperative Learning.

Outcome Based Education is based on the belief that all students can learn and learn well. OBE proclaims that equality should mean equality of outcomes rather than equality of opportunity. In order for the outcomes to be based on equality, the standard is lowered to ensure that all students, regardless of their ability, can reach the set standard.

In essence, the traditional subjects, way of teaching, and administration are thrown out the window. Traditional education, in order for a student to receive a diploma, says he must take a required number of courses such as four years of English, three years of mathematics, science, and social studies. In addition, two years of arts and humanities, a year of health and physical education, as well as several electives are also required. These traditional courses are called Carnegie Units.

According to Phyllis Schlafly, OBE replaces "academic work with attitudinal objective" and replaces "the traditional Carnegie Unit of measuring success with a nebulous arrangement in which the parents will never know what their children were taught."[6]

With Outcome Based Education, the student is required to achieve so many goals and "learning outcomes." In some states the requirement is fifteen goals and fifty-one "learning outcomes." Currently each state sets the required number of goals and "learning outcomes" that each student must achieve.

Several states such as Pennsylvania, Minnesota, New York, California, and Texas are seriously considering the implementation of Outcome Based Education. Among these states, Pennsylvania has been the model.

The March 11, 1992, issue of *Education Week* explains how the program has been proposed to work.

> The board would establish a set of skills and knowledge all students should attain, as well as assessment to measure students performance. Dis-

tricts would then develop strategic plans — which would have to be approved by the state board — outlining how they propose to enable students to acquire the learning outcomes. Students could then receive a diploma by demonstrating mastery of the outcomes, regardless of how many courses they took.[7]

Robert E. Feir, executive director of the Pennsylvania State Board of Education, has said, "the proposal is aimed at shifting the state's focus from regulating the process of education to setting goals for the outcomes of schooling."[8] Supposedly, these learning outcomes will be based on real life experiences, making a student's advancement from one grade to the next largely based on non-cognitive knowledge.

Conservative activist, Phyllis Schlafly, however, calls OBE, "an attempt to replace academic training with discussion of emotion, attitudes, and behavior. There is no accountability. Parents have no idea what the child is learning or what he has accomplished. It is an attempt to deceive parents about what is going on in the public school classroom."[9]

Why would professional educators want to keep parents in the dark about the material being taught to their child? The answer is easy: The liberal, humanistic educational (and political) establishment have a hidden agenda — the educational abduction of America's children. If you don't believe me, read on.

"Dumbing Down"

With Outcome Based Education, it is virtually impossible for anyone to fail. A student, who in traditional education would receive a D or F, is instead given an "incomplete" and the opportunity to retake the test or rework the assignment until they get at least 80 percent. Incompletes have no ill effects on a students grade point average (GPA). The end results are grade inflation and misleading class rankings.

In South Washington County, Minnesota, there are two

high schools and two junior high schools who service approximately 5,000 students. In 1992, under OBE, these four schools had 15,510 incompletes.[10] That's three incompletes for every student!

Students involved in the OBE experiment "are given the freedom to study at a rate, place, and time that is most convenient and effective for them and they progress only as fast as their personal ability permits."[11] That sounds nice, but as Dr. William Bennett, former secretary of education in the Reagan Administration, puts it, "The truth of the real world is that without standards and judgments, there can be no progress."[12]

Will the real world slow down and let the lazy or underachievers catch up or do it over and over until they get it right? Dr. S. Rimm, author of *The Under Achievement Syndrome: Cause and Cures,* makes this point: "Children who learn to lose without being devastated, and use failure to grow, will achieve in the classroom and society .... Children will become achievers only if they learn to function in competition."[13]

Competition, however, is no longer "politically correct" in many educational circles. In fact, one school district in Texas decided to stop presenting the valedictory and salutatory awards to the top two graduates each year because it created "too much competition." So what? Don't the young men and women who studied and achieved deserve to receive top honors? Is it fair to deny them public recognition for their efforts?

So, if competition in the classroom is eliminated, what do we have left? C. P. Yecke, writes in *OBE: The Work Ethic and Achievement,* that through Outcome Based Education, "the habit of laziness, procrastination, and irresponsibility are inculcated in students."[14] That's a pretty stinging indictment, but actual experience has proved it to be true.

One teenage girl who had been exposed to OBE for the past three years was interviewed on CBN's "700 Club" television program. She was asked by the interviewer, "Do you know where Europe is?"

Her embarrassed reply, "Sort of."

Then, after explaining Cooperative Learning, the reporter asked the girl, "How do you react when a few students in a work group do all the work and everybody in the group gets the same grade?"

"Well," she answered, "I used to try hard and do my best, but when I realized it didn't matter, I decided not to work any more either."

No wonder critics of OBE call it "dumbing down." Not only is competition discouraged but students get a second or third chance to master the vague, ill-defined goals described on their report cards[15] like:

- Respects self
- Respects right, opinions, and materials of others
- Makes productive decisions
- Works independently
- Works cooperatively in groups
- Accepts differences in people
- Demonstrates interest in learning
- Exhibits innovative thinking
- Speaks for a variety of purposes and audiences

I leave it up to your imagination as to how teachers will arrive at grading these illusive, undefined objectives.

What's more, the grading scale doesn't go from A to F. Students in this elementary school are given a check mark indicating:

— Consistently Evident
— Sometimes Evident
— Not Evident

You can bet it doesn't take long for kids to get wise to what's really going on. Like the teenage girl mentioned above, students will figure out the system and adjust accordingly. Come to think of it, maybe that's how you get a "Consistently Evident" grade in "Exhibits innovative thinking"!

Achieving Mediocrity

Let's look at a few of the fifty-one "learning outcomes" as listed by the Pennsylvania Department of Education. Notice the vagueness of the goals and the lack of cognitive knowledge.

> • All students understand and appreciate their worth as unique and capable individuals, and exhibit self-esteem.
> • All students relate in writing, speech, or other media, the history and nature of various forms of prejudice to current problems facing communities and nations, including the United States.
> • All students develop skills of communicating and negotiating with others to solve interpersonal problems and conflicts.
> • All students develop knowledge of physical fitness, including aerobic fitness and skills in lifetime sports and outdoor activities to promote lifelong physical activity.
> • All students relate basic human development theories to care giving and child care strategies.
> • All students apply the fundamentals of consumer behavior to managing available resources to provide for personal and family needs.
> • All students make environmentally sound decisions in their personal and civic lives.

Did you notice that the majority of these "learning outcomes" are based on attitudes, values, feelings, emotions, and political correctness?

When they *do* teach cognitive knowledge, however, the set standard or goal required for each grade level has been lowered so that everyone can learn and achieve.

For instance, in Outcome Based Education, the goal or standard of excellence is 80 percent. In the traditional way of teaching and testing, 80 percent is a C grade. In Outcome Based Education, 80 percent means you have mastered the subject! That means 80 percent is as good as receiving 100 percent. This is called grade inflation, and believe me, it is no accident.

Thomas Sowell in his book *Inside American Education,* discusses the fact that, in the last few years, we have seen a decline in academic performance, yet a rise in test scores.

> American high schools gave out approximately twice as many C's as A's in 1966, but by 1978 the A's actually exceeded the C's. By 1990, more than one-fifth of all entering freshmen in college averaged A minus or above for their entire high school careers. At private universities, entering freshmen with averages of A minus or above were an absolute majority — 54 percent . . . . These two trends — grade inflation and declining test scores — are by no means unconnected. Without the systematic deception of parents and the public by raising grades, it is highly unlikely that the decline in performance could have continued so long.[16]

Thomas Sowell makes the point that the educational establishment, in an effort to deceive parents and the public, hides the decline in educational achievement by lowering the standard for excellence and allowing students to receive better grades. This kind of numerical gymnastics is known as grade inflation.

The purpose of grade inflation is to make educational programs appear successful. As a result, the standard of excellence is really the standard of mediocrity. As with most programs supported by the liberal left, both social and economic, they strive to promote mediocrity not excellence.

According to William Bennett: "Improving American

education requires not doing new things but doing (and remembering) some good old things."[17]

When, Whether, or Never?

Traditional education is also outcome based in the true sense of the phrase. Students must meet set requirements in order to receive a passing grade in a subject or to move to the next grade level. To determine the difference between OBE and traditional education we must ask ourselves: What outcome are we looking for?

Do we want a student who has a firm foundation in the three R's, enjoys competing with himself and with others, gets all the facts in order to make an informed decision, is independent, and strives for excellence? Or do we want a student who whines when challenged, can't think for himself, expects others to lead him, goes with the flow and doesn't make waves, and is content to settle for something less than the best — mediocrity.

Both methods of teaching produce outcomes. Which student do you want your child to become?

The educational elite, however, prefer the politically correct "whiner." How do I know? Read this statement by William Spady, a nationally recognized supporter of Outcome Based Education as he describes the paradigm: "The OBE paradigm, or overview, is that *whether* students learn something is more important than *when* they learn it." Spady says our current view that "*when* students learn something is more important than *whether* they learn it well" is obsolete.[18]

In accordance with this mentality, one school district in Iowa has proposed a grading scenario that would score students with either A, B, or "not yet."

Sure, it's important that students learn the material. *When* they learn it, however, means they must discipline and apply themselves in order to master the material within an allotted period of time. Rules, regulations, and deadlines teach students about responsibility and how the real world operates. A student who can achieve within the boundaries set by his teachers can achieve in the real world.

Education should be based on the same principles that apply to the world in which the student will live and work as an adult. Allowing a student to learn the material when he wants — just as long as they learn it — is not how the real world operates.

Try telling your boss that it is not important whether you complete your current project by his set deadline just as long as you finish it. Most likely you'll find yourself looking for another job.

Spady's idea of Outcome Based Education resembles that of other liberals and educational elite. As usual the outcomes are not based on hard and fast cognitive knowledge. When will they realize that kids need outcomes that reflect a mastery of traditional academic subjects? Isn't that the purpose of the public schools — nothing more and nothing less? Only those who are out of touch with reality would disagree.

Mastery Learning

Madoline Hunter, author of *Mastery Learning,* has had a great deal of influence in the development of Outcome Based Education. While OBE is based on the testing of outcomes that are primarily non-cognitive, non-academic knowledge, mastery learning is just the opposite.

Mastery learning tests the outcomes of students based on cognitive knowledge. Sounds like a great program, right? Wrong.

Mastery learning does not use the traditional standard of testing and teaching. Instead, it sets a standard that each child must reach for every subject. For example, when it comes to geometry, every child must be tested to provide the needed data to demonstrate that the student has reached the required set standard of academic achievement.

What's wrong with this way of teaching and testing? In order for every child in a classroom to reach the set standard, it must be low enough to ensure that every student is capable of achieving it. If the standard is to high, those students who have learning disabilities will not be able to reach it.

As psychologist Steve Kossar, has said, "In order for everyone to slam dunk, you are going to have to lower the basket." Instead of encouraging a student to excel to his full potential, he is only encouraged to reach the required standard.

For example, Tommy fully understands the geometry lesson Mr. Johnson is teaching, and he is ready to move on to the next lesson. Regardless of this fact, Tommy is going to have to sit by and wait, along with most of the class, while Mr. Johnson tries to help Billy and a few others catch up. Billy, however, has a slight learning disability known as dyslexia. Dyslexia makes it difficult for Billy to understand abstract ideas like those presented in geometry.

So that Billy can graduate, he must reach the set academic standard in geometry. Billy, who really excels in biology, must take time away from the area where he excels to learn geometry well enough to reach the set academic standard. It would make great sense in Billy's case to transfer him into a basic accounting or general math class to obtain the needed math credits for graduation. Instead, Billy is forced to take geometry over and over in an attempt to meet the required standard.

In theory, Billy could be thirty years old and still in the tenth grade, trying to pass geometry. More than likely, Billy will just give up on attempting to reach the set standard. Instead of receiving a diploma, Billy will be given a certificate and be pushed aside as an academic failure.

This kind of narrow program does not encourage individuality nor does it encourage students to excel in the areas in which they are gifted. The student is either required to take time from those subjects in which he could excel in order to meet the required academic standard in a subject in which he has great difficulty, or the student is not permitted to excel past the set academic standard because class time is spent helping other students catch up.

Mastery learning is just another catchy phrase concocted by high-minded educators to achieve their ultimate goal: universal conformity.

Teach Less, Learn More?

Outcome Based Education creates another educational contradiction with the philosophy that less is more. The idea is: Teach the child less, and he will know more.

In a typical OBE math class, a child is asked by a teacher, "How do you get 32 plus 98?"

"You use a calculator," the student responds.

"Correct answer," the teacher replies.

This is no joke. In many math classes, students are no longer required to memorize number facts or learn mathematical procedures. If the calculator can provide the answer, all you have to know is how to use the calculator. That's how you get a "consistently evident" on your report card in "Uses a variety of problem-solving strategies" or "Uses mathematical strategies to calculate accurately."

In many states where Outcome Based Education exists, as in Minnesota, what was traditionally Spanish I is now Spanish I, II, and III.

In order to see that each and every child learns and excels, educators take what was traditionally taught a student in one year and teach it to him or her in three years. The idea is: Teach them less, and they will know more. They may know the basic material very well, but do they truly know more about the subject overall? Certainly not.

Teach them less, and they will know more is like saying concentrate on being stupid, and you will be intelligent.

Total Quality Management?

Like Outcome Based Education, another program called Total Quality Management, often referred to as TQM, has a list of desired outcomes. In fact, the main objective of TQM is the implementation of Outcome Based Education.

Introduced several years ago by W. Edward Demings, Total Quality Management was developed to increase productivity for corporations by teaching them who their customers are and how to best serve them by meeting their needs. From what we've learned about the educational establishment, however, these goals seem to contradict their master plan.

Indeed, the educational elite are not interested in true total quality management. Instead, they have taken a successful program with a good sounding name and borrowed a few buzz words in order to disguise their liberal program. If the educational elite were interested in true total quality management, they would strive to meet the needs and desires of their customers — the parents/taxpayers, but the educational elite could give two hoots about what you and I think.

Many manufacturers used TQM with great success. Part of the philosophy behind the program was to inspire employee participation. To do this, employers told their employees how important they are to the success of the company and that they desired their input. This made employees feel they had a say in the company and how the product was manufactured. As a result, a team attitude was created, making for greater productivity.

Even though employees supposedly had a lot of control over the manufacturing of the product, the boss made it very clear what he wanted the end result to be. For example, the boss might say, "I want your ideas on how we, as a team, can produce a more highly efficient, cost-effective, and quality ski boat. I don't care how we do it, but I want the end product to be a 19-foot, fiber glass ski boat with red leather interior, an AM/FM stereo with cassette player, 125-horse powered outboard motor with a blue stripe going along the outside of the boat."

The employees may have felt they had a lot of control in the process of manufacturing the boat, but the real power rested with the boss. Why? Because he controlled the outcome.

Well, if it worked for corporations, why not the educational system? Let's say you are in charge of the North Dakota Department of Instruction and you desire to implement a program into the schools , such as Outcome Based Education. You would more than likely face a lot of opposition if you ordered the implementation of Outcome Based Education.

But, if you said to your administrators, school boards, and superintendents, "We have decided to use a program that has been highly successful for corporations and manufacturers. Total Quality Management is a team approach to getting the job done. We want your ideas and input in developing the best educational system possible. To do that, we have come up with several goals and outcomes that we would like to achieve through this program. We don't care how you reach these goals and outcomes, but the end results must be consistent with these standards."

Such a scenario would enable you, as the state education board, to implement your desired program without a lot of opposition. Why? Because parents and taxpayers are duped into thinking they have a lot of control over the process. In actuality, they don't because the state has dictated what the outcome must be. And what is their desired program? Outcome Based Education, of course.

Dead in Its Tracks

Many state departments of education have implemented TQM, as well as Outcome Based Education without the permission of their state legislature. As a result, several congressmen are now drafting legislation making it mandatory to have such programs approved by the state legislature before they can be implemented. This would stop Outcome Based Education and TQM programs — that have already been implemented without prior approval of state legislatures — dead in their tracks.

As a result, committees would be formed to review and study the programs and their effectiveness or lack thereof. In addition, public hearings for parents and educators to express their likes and dislikes over such programs would be required. Such legislation would also give the owners of the schools — the taxpayers — the chance to voice their opinions about what their kids are taught. Taxpayers would have the opportunity to let their representatives know if they would like to have such programs in their schools or not.

After all, what gives state departments of education the right to implement such programs without your stamp of approval or disapproval? The fact of the matter is that the liberal educational elite could care less what you want. Their main interest is to implement any program that will give them more power and control for the purpose of promoting their philosophies and agenda.

Total Quality Management is just one way to disguise a controversial program under another name. Although TQM may help to implement such programs as Outcome Based Education, it will not create more quality in education.

Your Kids as Guinea Pigs?

Outcome Based Education is a poor choice for several reasons:

1. OBE lowers the standard of education by lowering the standard of academic achievement.
2. OBE infringes on parental authority by teaching and imposing values, such as values clarification.
3. OBE takes away parental control at the local level due to the states over involvement with pre-set outcomes.
4. *OBE has the possibility to be extremely expensive.*

Parents and legislators in Pennsylvania have been fighting against the proposed "educational reform" being jammed down their throats by the State Board of Education. Despite state-wide objection by an angry public and refusal by some districts to implement OBE, the State Board of elite educationalists think they know what is best for Pennsylvania's children.

Pennsylvania parents, however, don't want their children used as "guinea pigs" in an already failed and expensive experiment. How do they know it has failed? The evidence speaks for itself.

In a flyer distributed by the Pennsylvania Christian Coalition,[19] the negative results of OBE on student progress were noted:

> **The Chicago School District:** After years in the system, ninth graders could not derive the meaning from what they read! Parents in Chicago started referring to these schools as "Factories of Failure." Finally, parents filed a law suit calling the whole thing, "Educational Malpractice."

> **Arkansas:** After three years, scores dropped in eleven out of twelve grade levels, while the twelfth one remained the same.

> **Alberta and British Columbia, Canada:** Newspapers reported that students "lost two years of their educational lives. . . They have been guinea pigs in what increasingly appears a failed experiment." They spent millions of taxpayers dollars to find out this experiment doesn't work.

In spite of the overwhelming evidence that Outcome Based Education is a fluke, Pennsylvania and other states are forging ahead. Why? Do the educational elite have something besides education on their minds?

6

School:
The Surrogate Parent?

One parent described Outcome Based Education as, "Clearly an effort to create societal change through classroom education." What does that mean? That schools will no longer center on academics; instead they will seek to mold kids in social areas. Someone has called it, "Red, white, and blue socialism."

One distraught parent whose children had been taught under OBE said, "I feel like I'm sending my kids to prison." Why? Because she realized that teachers were using the same mind-control techniques practiced by totalitarian societies.

Like Russia's old Red Guard communists, OBE proponents strive to replace parents as authority figures for their kids. "We teachers have to take responsibility for raising your kids," one educator stated bluntly.

An angry parent, aware of OBE's dangers, said, "Our children are being victimized" and noted that "OBE curriculum encourages suicide."

Another parent, interviewed on CBN's "700 Club," reported that prostitutes had been brought into her child's class to share about life "on the street." When the mother asked why this had been allowed, she was told, "To show kids that the values they are being taught at home are not necessarily the only way of looking at things."

What's going on? I believe the promoters of Outcome Based Education have two related objectives on their agenda. One is to prepare America's children for a socialized nation dominated by a world view that denies nationalism and morality. Because they know most Americans object to such thinking, the education elite must wrench control of the schools out of the hands of local school boards and parents. How will they do that?

First, those students who continually do not meet the "politically correct" outcomes will be re-educated, or re-mediated. It troubles me to think how many Christian kids will be persecuted for holding on to their biblical beliefs and family instilled values.

In order to obtain this first objective of controlling the thinking of America's children, educators must be in a position to dictate what kids are taught. How do they purpose to do that? By presenting high-minded "educational goals" in an effort to dupe parents and then slipping their new curriculum into place, hoping no one will notice.

You can bet, however, once Outcome Based Education gets its big foot in the door, it won't go away without a fight. In fact, the real outcome will be more and more state and federal interference in local schools.

How do we know that? Because of what is already taking place in districts where OBE is in operation. Whenever local school boards complain that they are losing control, OBE proponents pooh-pooh their fears with: It will "be up to the districts to assess student outcomes, while the state will assess districts every three years."[1] The supporters of OBE call this "local control."

How much control does a school have when they are handed the outcomes and told that they can achieve them in any way they choose just as long as they achieve them? What happens if the state rejects the plan your district has developed for achieving the set outcomes? That means back to the drawing board and more money spent on developing a "corrective action plan" that will meet state requirements.

The Michigan Model:
Assuming the Role of Parents

Where did Outcome Based Education come from? First introduced in Michigan, OBE began as a state-sponsored comprehensive school health curriculum in 1984.

Several million dollars from federal, state, and local sources were used to develop the nine volumes of the Model curriculum, with more than 2,500 pages, covering 863 different student learning objectives for children between five and thirteen years old.

To determine the Michigan Model's effectiveness, a Senate Select Committee was formed. Their findings were shocking and confirm what many parents already knew to be true.

Republican Senators Gil Dinello, Doug Carl, Bob Geake, and Democratic Senator Jim Berryman sat on the Senate Select Committee to study the Michigan Model for Comprehensive School Health Education. Remember, regardless of what they call it, it is nothing less than Outcome Based Education.

Senator Gil Dinello, chairman of the Select Committee had this to say in the preface of the Senate report:

> From the hearings we held around the state, it became clear that the social engineers, the social reconstruction that exists at the higher levels of the education profession, stepped in to make the local school the surrogate parent. Their attitude was that the school was the venue where children should be equipped to deal with life's situations, including such intimate areas as sexuality and social decision making. The Michigan Model

attempts to place teachers in the undesirable role
of having to cross these boundaries that were
previously recognized as the responsibility of the
family.

Why do the schools feel they need to take over the
responsibilities of the parents? Because we, the owners of the
schools, allowed them to do so a little at a time. We trusted
them because they were the "experts."

In his book, *The Devaluing of America,* William Bennett
spells out the attitude of the educational establishment: "The
common sense view of parents and the public, that schools
reinforce rather than undermine the values of home, family,
and country, was increasingly rejected."

Senator Gil Dinello provides the antidote to OBE's
interference in family life:

> Parents need to re-examine themselves and
> be vigilant in how they perform as the first and
> most important teacher of their children. They
> need to adjust their interaction with their children
> until they are full-fledged participants in equip-
> ping their children to cope with a society that is
> fixated on sex, substance abuse, materialism, low
> commitment levels, and an emphasis on self.
>
> Government is not equipped to raise your
> children. It can complement what you do. But left
> unchecked it can also compete. Parents hold the
> key. Committed involvement with their children's
> education will tip the scales towards the family.[2]

Good advice, but "committed involvement" with your
child's education takes determination and persistence as the
parents in Michigan discovered.

The Senate Select Committee's report on the Michigan
Model found many things wrong with the program. Because
these findings would be consistent with any Outcome Based

Education program, let's examine each one carefully.

Finding Number One: *Michigan Departments of Education and Public Health organized a campaign to discredit concerned parents.*

These state agencies had the Michigan Model enacted without a vote from the Michigan Senate or House. The four senators who sat on the Senate Select Committee found that top officials from the Department of Education and Public Health used taxpayer funds to hold training sessions around the state for local school officials on how to discredit Michigan Model opponents. The senators reported that they "have the dates, times, places, the names of those who participated, and what they were told."

The strategy of the Michigan Model Steering Committee was simple: Any parent or teacher who got in the way of implementing the Michigan Model at a local school district was to be labeled as a right wing, fundamentalist Christian fanatic. The education establishment painted a picture of that person that would qualify as slander in any court of law. The goal was to squash the opposition at any cost and in any way.

Finding Number Two: *The state of Michigan has fallen short in supporting families and family values.*

The report stated: "Children should not be viewed alone as clients of the state, but should be viewed as members of a family unit. We feel that the traditional family is alive and still a vital force in our society, but its condition is wobbly. Its condition has been dramatically affected by the 'me-first' philosophy."

Finding Number Three: *Parents are being denied choice about Michigan Model and non-directive affective ed classes.*

"We listened to hundreds of parents tell about their efforts to have their children excused from non-sex ed Michigan Model classes. These parents were made, in most instances, to walk a bureaucratic maze that would confound and stupefy the most experienced special interest lobbyist. There needs to be a strong statement that parents are the number one decision makers for their children. It's a foundational principle that schools need to respect."

As one mother from Northville, Michigan, said:

> If Bible-based morality is prohibited then so should this relative morality. Because of my serious objections to the Michigan Model . . . I requested that my child be excused from Health Class in accordance with my rights per Michigan Compiled Law. During a meeting with the assistant superintendent, to discuss my right in accordance with the law, I was told, in essence, that the board was above the law. Further, she advised that if I continued to take my child out of Health Class each week that she would consider calling Protective Services!
>
> What on earth happened to our system or even the local government that would allow an assistant superintendent to tell me that I have no authority over what my child is taught? And, further, why would our elected school board members permit her to speak for them in regard to being above the law? Why should I have to pay for a legal defense when there are laws already on the books that address these issues? I am a parent, and a tax-paying one at that. Where are my rights? Elected board members: Where are you? What do I do now . . . call the police department?[3]

Finding Number Four: *Parents are without representation at local school level.*

These senators "observed that through the testimony of many board members and school administrators that the local school board is no longer the parent's/taxpayer's liaison to public education on the local level. In reality, the local school board has come to represent the school administration and not parents and families. On paper, parents have the local school board to represent them. But in reality, they are without representation in local school matters."[4]

Finding Number Five: *Because of mixed messages about pre-marital sex, Michigan Model lessons result in increased adolescent sexual promiscuity.*

"Michigan Model teachers tell their students out of one side of their mouth that they should abstain from pre-marital sexual intercourse and out of the other they tell students how to be safe if they decide to have sex. It's a mixed message that rings loud and clear through the ears of teenagers whose hormones are moving at breakneck speed."[5]

The committee recommended that legislation be passed that mandates abstinence from pre-marital sexual activity as the basis for sex education. A few of the expected outcomes, according to the Senate Select Committee, should be:

1. Compare and contrast human procreation and animal reproduction. We need to teach our kids that they are human beings with the ability to say no, and to treat sex as something special between two married people. Our kids are not animals who do not think, but just react. Yet, that is how we treat them.

2. Explain the physical, emotional, and psychological risks associated with premarital sexual activity.

3. Examine the physical, emotional, and psychological benefits to a teen lifestyle free from genital-arousing activity.

4. Describe various ways for teens to say no to sex.

5. List some of the responsibilities of parenthood.

6. Explain why adoption is a healthy alternative to abortion.

7. Realize that true sexual freedom includes the freedom to say no to sex outside of marriage.

Finding Number Six: *"Calm-breathing" could be hazardous to your child's health.*

"Many of the breathing exercises, indeed, resemble the

mystical elements of Eastern religions. There is not only a breach of the church and state separation, but there is a lack of acknowledgment that an altered state of consciousness can be induced through breathing. Used by an inexperienced teacher, such exercises can produce hypnotic states in some children."[6]

Finding Number Seven: *Many in the educational community treat parents with arrogance and mistrust.*

"There is a pervasive attitude among many administrators and health educators that they know best what children need. They communicate to parents that they are the professionals and the parents are the unschooled amateurs. This is an attitude which must be squashed."[7]

Finding Number Eight: *The core problem facing Michigan schools is a moral one. All other problems derive from it.*

"Our students are not learning self-discipline and respect for others through the Michigan Model. As long as this continues, they will continue to exploit each other sexually. As the August 21 edition of *USA Weekend* states: 'If they don't learn courage and justice, curriculums to improve self-esteem won't stop the epidemic of extortion, bullying, and violence.'"[8]

Finding Number Nine: *Efforts to curb teen pregnancies and teen abortions was hindered by Michigan Model lessons.*

"At each hearing site, it became obvious that the state of Michigan is teaching our kids it's okay to get pregnant. Of course, the health educators would deny it. They would retort, they support abstinence, but if children are 'going to do it' then they should have all the right information to make the correct decisions. Mixed messages lead to the attitude that anything goes."[9]

Finding Number Ten: *Boundaries between church and state were violated with New Age teachings.*

"It was a common refrain in much of the testimony we heard around the state. A large number of parents felt that many of the Michigan Model basics contained New Age teachings. At first blush, it's really hard to see how one can see Eastern mysticism, the occult, or the New Age in any of the lessons in the curriculum.

"By listening to hundreds of parents and reading their letters, the committee started to see a troubling pattern emerge. New Age is there. It's in the Michigan Model. It's there under the guise of something else. Relaxation techniques, mini-vacations, calm-breathing, problem-solving, values clarification, yoga, and meditation. What does this mean? It means that our so-called state-sponsored, state-supported curriculum that purports to be value free, actually promotes religious practices. And it promotes religious practices subscribed to by a minority of people in this state and country."

Conclusion

The report concluded by saying that "the child is first and foremost a member of a family. The child has a natural claim to a two-parent family. Any policy that does not recognize this claim and does not strengthen the family is not pro-family or pro-child. The Michigan Model fails miserably in this regard."[10]

The Final, Fatal Outcome

Hear this and hear it good: The Michigan Model is nothing less than a form of Outcome Based Education.

Some people question whether the Michigan Model is a form of Outcome Based Education because its lists of outcomes are health oriented. Let me ask: How do you define health education?

Traditional health education normally consists of reproduction, personal hygiene, and diet. I do not call sex education based on values clarification and the promotion of New Age techniques traditional health education.

The Michigan Model is, without a doubt, a form of Outcome Based Education. You can call a truck a car, but it is still a truck. You can call the Michigan Model a health course if you want, but it is a form of OBE.

Don't be fooled. Other educational models are now in the process of being implemented in many states. The names are different, but the philosophies are the same. In fact, according to the Rutherford Institute, 31 states are now involved at various levels with the OBE program.

Currently Senator Gilbert J. Dinello is drafting seventeen pieces of legislation that call for major changes to the Michigan Model. The senator is truly fighting for the traditional family.

Unfortunately, Outcome Based Education will continue to be promoted and implemented for four reasons:

1. Outcome Based Education is an attempt to teach our kids relativism and political correctness.

Is there any doubt why America's school children are continuing to fall behind other students all over the world? While Japanese students are studying math, science, and other courses of academic value, America's students are being taught and tested on a wide range of politically correct principles and positions.

It is not the job of the state to teach, test, and evaluate the personal beliefs and convictions of students. The only job of the educational system is to teach our kids to read, write, and do arithmetic. The rest of the educational process belongs to the parents.

2. Outcome Based Education will help to give liberals more and lasting power.

Why? Because Outcome Based Education spends an overwhelming amount of time on attitudes, values, feelings, and emotions instead of stressing true cognitive and academic knowledge. As a result, we will end up with graduates who are not prepared to enter into an ever increasingly competitive work force. Many individuals, because of the lack of a quality education, will be unqualified for high-paying jobs. An increase in low-income individuals and families will create more individuals who are dependent on the government for handouts. Most liberals gain their power and support from those who are dependent on their social programs. This is one main reason why liberals stay in positions of power.

3. Outcome Based Education makes it impossible to judge whether a teacher is doing his or her job adequately.

Because little cognitive material is taught, there is little cognitive knowledge to measure. As test scores continue to decline, many teacher unions will support Outcome Based Education in an effort to make it nearly impossible to gauge teachers' effectiveness in the classroom. This program hides the failure of an entire educational system and its leaders — the educational elite.

For example, take a teacher who is responsible to educate a group of children. If, at the end of the year, the majority of these kids cannot read, perform arithmetic, or pick out the United States on a world map, this teacher's failure and lack of ability to teach would soon be discovered. The tests based on the cognitive knowledge that he or she was responsible to teach would provide conclusive evidence of the teacher's incompetence.

If, however, you teach and test those children on subjects that are vague, subjective, and based on attitudes, values, feelings, and emotions, instead of hard academic, cognitive knowledge, then there is no way you can gauge whether a child has learned anything. At the same time, there is no way to determine if a teacher has failed in his or her responsibility. No wonder this program is so popular with many teachers and their unions.

4. And finally, Outcome Based Education will be implemented because some people actually think it will benefit America's students.

What will be the outcome of Outcome Based Education? We will end up with more American children who lack skills in reading, writing, and arithmetic, as well as the ability to tell right from wrong. However, they will most certainly be able to distinguish between what is considered politically correct and incorrect.

The Law Is on Your Side

Is this what you want for your children? If not, you can fight OBE.

First of all, parents should exercise their rights and refuse to allow their children to be subjected to psychological testing and treatment. This right is guaranteed under the Hatch Amendment passed in 1978, which requires that parents must give their consent before any child in a state school can be given psychiatric, psychological, behavioral testing, or questioning.

The Hatch Amendment, however, was basically not enforced until the Moral Majority, the Heritage Foundation, Eagle Forum, and the Committee for the Survival of a Free Congress put pressure on the Reagan Administration to appoint Dr. William Bennett as secretary of education to enforce the Hatch Amendment.

Even if Outcome Based Education promoted the philosophies of most Christian conservatives, our children would still not be receiving a good education. Instead, they would be preoccupied with something other than the primary purpose of education: the teaching of basic and fundamental concepts, such as reading, writing, and arithmetic.

In fact, you have a constitutional right to raise and educate your children as you see fit. Several cases decided by the Supreme Court of the United States have made parental rights clear time and time again.

In 1923, in the case of *Meyer* v. *Nebraska,* the Supreme Court affirmed the right of parents to place their children in Lutheran schools taught in German: "It is the natural duty of the parent to give his children education suitable to their station in life."[11]

The case of *Pierce* v. *Society of Sisters* (1925) responded to a 1922 Oregon statute requiring each school-age child to attend public schools. The court decided that "the Act of 1922 unreasonably interferes with the liberty of parents and guardians to direct the upbringing and the education of children under their control." In addition, the Justices said, "Fundamental . . . liberty . . . excludes any general power of the state to standardize its children. . . . The child is not the mere creature of the state; those who nurture him . . . have the right . . . to recognize and prepare him for additional obligations."[12]

Wisconsin v. *Yoder* (406 U.S. 205, 1972) supported the Amish community's refusal to send their children to school beyond eighth grade, noting that the effects of the compulsory attendance law would be to compel them to violate their religious principles and destroy the value system underlying the Amish community. The High Court stated, "Any conflict between public schooling and a family's basic and sincerely held values interferes with the family's First Amendment Rights."[13]

You can fight state and federal implementation of Outcome Based Education with confidence. The law is on your side! Get the facts, go to your local school board meetings, and let your voice be heard!

Why is this battle against OBE so important?

Former Vice-President Dan Qualye, in his acceptance speech at the Republican Convention in August of 1992, made it clear:

> Americans try to raise their children to understand right and wrong only to be told that every so-called lifestyle alternative is morally equivalent. That is wrong. The gap between us and our opponents is a cultural divide. It is not just a difference between conservative and liberal, it is a difference between fighting for what is right and refusing to see what is wrong.

The battle may be tough and ugly and bloody, but we must never forget why we are fighting: for the hearts and minds — and very lives — of America's children.

7

Values Clarification: No Right or Wrong

Years ago, I heard a statement and wrote it in my Bible: "Wrong is wrong even if everybody is doing it, and right is right even if no one is doing it."

Today, the proponents of values clarification curriculum would consider the above statement outdated and irrational.

Two of the major supporters of values clarification, Sidney Simon and Lawrence Kohlberg, believe that "moral education has amounted to little more than an attempt by elders to 'impose' values upon the young. They claim to offer something different, and better. In fact, what they offer is different, but certainly no better."[1]

What they offer is "values clarification" courses that tell kids there are no moral absolutes. The constantly recurring theme is: You must decide for yourself what is right and wrong.

William Bennett in *The Public Interest, Moral Education in the Schools*, writes:

Kohlberg has said that "traditional moral

education . . . [is] undemocratic and unconstitutional." Instead of teaching morals to children,
Kohlberg stresses the need for a new psychology
and a new philosophy that recognizes "the child's
right to freedom from indoctrination." Adults are
to view the child not as a pupil but as a "moral
philosopher" in his own right. This, he says,
"reflects a 'progressive ideology' with a 'liberal,
democratic and non-indoctrinative' notion of education."[2]

How does this "progressive ideology" work? William
Bennett describes the consequences:

People are bundles of wants; the world is a
battlefield of conflicting wants; and no one has
room for goodness, decency, or the capacity for a
positive exercise of will. Moral maturity is certainly not to be found in the clarification of values,
which is cast solely in the language of narrow self-
gratification and is devoid of any considerations
of decency whatsoever. Finally and ironically,
Simon's approach emphatically indoctrinates —
by encouraging and even exhorting the student to
narcissistic self-gratification.[3]

The results of this kind of amoral and even immoral
teaching can have a devastating effect on young, impressionable minds.

Drug Prevention?

Many supposed health or anti-drug and alcohol curriculum are based on the controversial "values clarification"
approach.

In 1988 the United States Department of Education
published a booklet titled, *Drug Prevention Curricula*. This
book accurately described what values clarification courses
are really all about:

Curricula which emphasizes open-ended decision making about using dangerous substances should likewise be rejected. Many curricula marketed are based on the controversial "values clarification" approach to teaching students decision making skills and ethical standards. Values clarification is a strategy that avoids leading the student to any particular conclusion, relying instead upon the child's inner feelings and logic to develop a set of values that are consistent with those embraced by the culture at large.[4]

Studies show that drug and alcohol abuse actually tend to rise after students go through such a class. And no wonder. After weeks and months of discussion on how to use drugs, how they make you feel, and how to get them, a child's natural curiosity is dramatically raised. At the same time, since no conclusions about what is right or wrong are permitted, what's to keep kids from experimenting with these dangerous substances?

Today's relativistic society proclaims there is no absolute right and wrong, no good or evil; there is only interaction of forces. Yet, they contradict this belief by stating that the only absolute is your own reasoning.

This is exactly what Satan, in the form of a serpent, told Eve in the Garden of Eden, "And you shall know good from evil, [relativism in morality]" (Gen. 3:5).

Another name for this deception is situational ethics. This system of ethics judges acts within their context instead of by categorical principles. The proponents of situational ethics maintain it is very difficult to have a pre-determined set of values. Instead, each individual must take into account — with each situation — the time, place, and events surrounding each circumstance. Once this has been done, you can make your decision based on what the best results or outcome would be regardless of what is morally right or wrong.

Many of today's school children are receiving a daily

dose of this humanistic teaching under the guise of health, anti-drug, or alcohol classes. With little adult guidance, no wonder kids put themselves in life threatening situations.

The Rule, Not the Exception

During the summer of 1990, in Montgomery County, Maryland, a group of teenagers blew their minds on the hallucinogenic drug LSD.

A *Washington Post* reporter spent the night with these teens, observing and taking notes while these minor children broke the law by popping four, five, and six hits of acid. The reporter made no attempt to stop the kids or to offer any moral advice. Afterward, the young teens described their hallucinations, which included faces appearing in the woodwork, paper bursting into flames, images in the mirror turning into devils.

When this reporter wrote up her story, she concealed the identities of the teens involved.

Public reaction to the reporter's story generated immediate outrage. Many people felt that it was not right for this reporter to sit by and watch these minor children take dangerous and illegal drugs. Shouldn't she have called the police? Or shouldn't she have contacted each child's parent(s) so they could seek some help for their child?

The out-cry and response was so great that the *Washington Post* had Richard Hoarwood, one of their best writers, take on the task of answering the letters and calls of criticism. In his written response, which was published in the *Washington Post*, Hoarwood said, "In a business with no fixed moral or ethical formula, their ethics just get invented as [they] go along." In other words, the end justifies the means. It matters not how you get the story, just as long as you get it.

Hoarwood went on to say, "Ethics is not even [a] concern." That means situational ethics is not the exception, but the rule.

Our children need to be taught right from wrong, not to be led through a process of weighing what is the best outcome for them in any given circumstance.

In a scene from the movie, *The Witness*, Harrison Ford plays a government agent. Wounded, he is taken into the home of an Amish family. One day, rising from his sick bed, Ford catches the family's eight year old reaching for Ford's loaded pistol. What is his response?

The agent yells: "Samuel! Never, ever play with a loaded gun!"

Samuel is not asked how he feels about what he's doing; nor is an offer made to teach him a four-step, decision-making model. Getting him to make up his own mind about whether loaded guns are dangerous is not what the situation demands.

Instead, a knowledgeable adult leads the boy through an exercise in single-trial learning. As the *Journal of Adolescent Counseling* states concerning the movie incident: "It is clear at the end of the subsequent conversation between them that the boy has learned. He is unlikely to forget what he must never, ever do."

Sounds reasonable since this is how most parents deal with their children about potentially harmful activities. Educators, however, take a radically different approach.

Clarified Wants and Desires

Sidney Simon and Louis E. Raths, state the goal of values clarification in their book, *Values Clarification*: "To involve students in practical experiences making them aware of their own feelings, their own ideas, their own beliefs, so that the choices and decisions they make are conscious and deliberate, based on their own value systems."[5]

How does this idea affect the parent-child relationship? Richard A. Baer, Jr., in an article published in the *Wall Street Journal* titled, "Parents, Schools, and Values Clarification," wrote:

> The originators of values clarification simply assume that their own subjective theory of values is correct . . . . If parents object to their children using pot or engaging in premarital sex,

the theory behind values clarification makes it appropriate for the child to respond, "But that's just your value judgment. Don't force it on me."[6]

Rolf Zetterson, vice-president of Focus on the Family, tells about a personal experience he had with educators over values clarification:

> I attended a recent parent-teacher conference at the school district where our two children attend. The purpose of this meeting was to provide parents with the opportunity to review new curriculum being introduced to the district. The district staff explained the basic philosophies behind the proposed material. The first principle shocked me. "Henceforth," they said, "teachers will not be responsible for giving students the right answers."
>
> "Wait a minute," I interrupted. "Can you tell me what you mean by that?"
>
> The panel of "experts" then told me how they had come to this conclusion on the basis of years of educational research: "First, we have found that what is true today may not be true tomorrow. It would be presumptuous for our instructors to push today's reality down the throats of their pupils. Second, we feel that what is truth to you may not be truth to me. It is all relative. Third, we know we can severely damage a child's self-esteem by telling him he has the wrong answer."[7]

That reminds me of a cartoon I saw in *USA Weekend* magazine. A teacher who had been called in by the principal stands in front of his desk, explaining, "I socialized them, I affirmed them, and I validated their self-esteem . . . . I didn't have *time* to teach them anything."[8]

William Bennett, former secretary of education under the Reagan Administration has said, "The 'values clarification' movement didn't clarify values, it clarified wants and desires. This form of moral relativism said, in effect, that no set of values was right or wrong; everybody had an equal right to his own values; and all values were subjective, relative, personal."[9]

In his book *The Devaluing of America,* Dr. Bennett goes on to report that in 1985, the *New York Times* published an article quoting New York area educators, in slavish devotion to this new view, proclaiming that "they deliberately avoid trying to tell students what is ethically right and wrong."[10]

But does this kind of thinking actually affect the way teachers teach in the classroom? Absolutely!

During one of my "The Traditional Family's Quest for Survival" Seminars, a parent in South Dakota brought me the teacher's manual to a book titled, *Personal and Social Responsibility,* by Constance Demborsky and published by an organization called Effective Skill Development for Adolescence.

Turning to page 46, this concerned mother pointed to a paragraph.

I read what the teacher was instructed to say to the students: "You see there is no way you can do this activity wrong. In fact, there is no way that you can do any activity in this class wrong. I hope one of the learnings that you take with you from this course is that there is no way to do life wrong."[11]

Again on page 63, the teacher was instructed to tell the class, "There is no way to do it — anything — wrong. Knowing that there is no way to do it wrong . . . gives you permission to do something new — to risk."[12]

No wonder kids today are so confused. At home parents try to teach them right from wrong while teachers at school tell them there is no right or wrong. During impressionable and often rebellious teenage years, whom do you think kids would prefer to believe?

Children of the Rainbow?

To make matters worse, the educational propagandists don't stop at just letting the students make up their own set of rules to live by. They go beyond and push their own agenda. How do they attempt to do that? Let me provide a recent example.

In New York City, the debate over the "Children of the Rainbow" curriculum revolved around three controversial books: *Daddy's Roommate, Heather Has Two Mommies,* and *Gloria Goes to Gay Pride.* These books are on the recommended reading list for first graders in New York City public schools.

In the December 14, 1992, issue of *Time* magazine, an article called, "Jack and Jack and Jill and Jill," had this to say about the content of one of the books:

> *Daddy's Roommate* is a congenial children's book about a boy in a not-so-unusual position; his parents have divorced. The rest of his story is a bit more unconventional. His father is living with a new companion named Frank. The boy is told by his mother that "Daddy and Frank are gay . . . being gay is just one more kind of love."[13]

First graders who turn the pages will learn that the two men live together. They "eat together." And one other thing. They "sleep together."

A quote from the first grade book, *Gloria Goes to Gay Pride,* says, "Some women love women. Some men love men. Some women and men love each other. That's why we march in the parade, so everyone can have a choice."[14]

In addition, the curriculum demands that teachers make students aware "of the changing concept of family in today's society. . . . Classes should include references to lesbians, gay people, in all curricular areas."[15]

After much investigation and listening to parent complaints, District Board President Mary Cummins publicly vowed not to implement the 443-page curriculum that New York Schools Chancellor Joseph Fernandez had developed as a result of a 1989 policy on multicultural education.

What was the outcome? Let me explain.

New York's decentralized system has 32 community school districts, each with a nine-member board that controls all elementary and middle schools in their area. A spokesman for Chancellor Fernandez said that out of the 32 districts, eight accepted the curriculum as is. The rest tinkered with the controversial sections, voting to either delete or delay them until later grades.

When Mary Cummins and the district's other members refused the entire document, Chancellor Fernandez fired them. The Board of Education, however, eventually reinstated them. The chancellor's spokesmen then said that the curriculum could be ignored as long as local boards devise a way to adhere to the Board of Education's policy on multicultural education. A few months later, in February, Chancellor Fernandez himself was fired.

In the next election, Mary Cummins was overwhelmingly re-elected. In fact, she was the top vote-getter in her district with three times more votes than any other school board candidate. In addition, ten of the 32 community school boards now have pro-family majorities — up from three before the election.[16] In stating her position, grandmother and District board president, Mary Cummins, said, "I will not demean legitimate minorities, such as blacks, Hispanics, Asians, whatever, by lumping them together with homosexuals. Homosexuals do not come under a racial or ethnic minority."

According to an article in *USA Today*, Howard Hurwitz, chairman of the Family Defense Council of New York City, sees the increase in use of curriculum on sexual orientation as "a national problem. Hurwitz says, "It's not sex education at all, it's sex titillation."[17] Hurwitz goes on to say, "I'm no homophobic in the sense that I give a hoot . . . what the individual homosexual is doing with his life. But I am concerned for what they are doing in the schools."[18]

Ruth Messinger, the Manhattan Borough president, who appeared on ABC's "Nightline" in 1992 to argue in favor of this curriculum, proclaimed that such material is necessary because these issues are on the minds of first graders.[19]

The only way the subject of homosexual/lesbian lifestyles and relationships occupies the thinking of first graders is when someone deliberately puts the topic before them. And even then, I doubt they can understand what it really means.

What is on the minds of first graders? The same subjects that have always been on the minds of children in the first grade: lunch and recess.

One-Sided Tolerance

The educational elite who write and promote such perverted propaganda *want* young children to think about the topic of homosexual/lesbian lifestyles. Why? Their goal is to desensitize and educate an entire generation in the belief that such lifestyles are normal and acceptable. In order to develop to do this, they must start with the youngest and most impressionable children under their authority — the first graders.

In the words of Brooks Alexander:

> In the ideological contest for cultural supremacy, public education is the prime target; it influences the most people in the most pervasive way at the most impressionable age. No other social institution has anything close to the same potential for mass indoctrination.[20]

The proposed purpose of the curriculum, "Children of the Rainbow," according to the article in *Time* magazine, was "to foster respect for all races, ethnic groups, and religions."[21]

Did you catch that? Respect for religions? Since when have educators been interested in teaching children respect for the traditional Judeo Christian religious system? Our kids are taught — through multiculturalism — to understand and accept the culture and religion of the Hindu, Buddhist, and Moslem. But let a child or a Christian teacher try to sing a Christmas carol or post a picture of a manger scene, and the school administration will call out the ACLU!

The elite in education consider themselves to be open-minded because they love everybody and are accepting of other people, cultures, and lifestyles. Yet, out the other side of their mouths, they ridicule the traditional family, traditional values, and traditional sex roles. In fact, in the original wording of the "Children of the Rainbow" curriculum, teachers were urged to encourage first graders "to view lesbians/gays as real people to be respected and appreciated."[22]

How can they say they are accepting of other lifestyles and religions when they won't even permit the Bible to be a part of education, even from a historical point of view? After all, the Bible is not only a great piece of historical literature, it is the foundation of Judeo Christian religion and values on which our country was founded. For generations, Christianity has been the major religion of our country. Yet, today, the Bible is not permitted in the classroom. A book on Zen-Buddhism? No problem, but don't even consider carrying a Bible in your book bag.

To the educational elite I say, "Don't tell me you want to foster respect and acceptance for all lifestyles and religions when you won't even teach traditional Judeo Christian history. In fact, you go out of your way to promote acceptance and respect for other religions and lifestyles that are diametrically opposed to the Judeo Christian faith."

Whenever certain lifestyles or religions are presented in a classroom to the neglect of others, in essence, the teacher is saying that any other way of life or belief is not important and does not merit acceptance or respect. Thus the educational system promotes an attitude of nonacceptance and disrespect for other lifestyles and religions — the very attitude they are supposedly against.

Sir Walter Moberly said: "It is a fallacy to suppose that by omitting a subject you teach nothing about it. On the contrary, you teach that it is to be omitted, and therefore a matter of secondary importance."[23]

Buddha but Not Bibles

Rush Limbaugh in his book, *The Way Things Ought to Be,* sums up the problem in American education today:

> I can think of no single action that would be better . . . than letting someone back into our schools that liberals would probably call a dead white man. I'm talking about God. Think about it. We now teach kids to use condoms, we instruct them in multiculturalism, we tell them lies about American history, and yet we can't teach them the Ten Commandments. We can't teach 'Thou Shalt Not Steal,' 'Thou Shalt Not Kill.' This is nothing less than depriving children of their moral and mental nutrients during their formative years.[24]

What happened to the Ten Commandments? "On November 17, 1980, the Supreme Court struck down a Kentucky law that required the posting of the Ten Commandments in the public school classroom."[25] That decision set a precedent for the removal of all Christian documents and biblical mandates from the walls of American schoolrooms.

Some of the same Supreme Court justices who made this decision, however, daily sit below a large chiseled copy of the Ten Commandments. Over the etching hovers a great American eagle as if protecting the hallowed words from the Book of Exodus.

Too bad these Supreme Court justices didn't remember the decision of an 1892 Court ruling that stated, "Our civilization and our institutions are infallibly Christian." One hundred years later, the Ten Commandments are considered contraband material and illegal propaganda too sinister for display in America's classrooms.

In fact, in 1992, the Supreme Court refused to review a

tragically misguided lower court ruling. The Colorado State Supreme Court, in the case of *Roberts* v. *Madigan*, had banned the Bible from a public school classroom. To make matters worse, that same ruling said it was perfectly acceptable for a public school teacher to have a book about Buddha on his desk — but not the Bible!

Why not? Because the Bible demands adherence to a strict set of values that leaves no room for clarification. No wonder the liberals and the educationalists want it banned!

Is it any wonder, then, that we are seeing an ever increasing rise in rape, murder, robbery, auto theft, and mugging? Today's children are being taught that there is no right or wrong; nothing is considered good or evil; everything is relative; there is only interaction of forces. Values clarification promotes the idea that there are no absolutes. Each individual must decide for himself or herself what is acceptable or unacceptable behavior, according to each situation they encounter.

God help us.

8

Quest International: Keeping Parents in the Dark

Whenever I conduct one of my seminars, "The Traditional Family's Quest for Survival," inevitably, a parent will approach me and ask about *Quest International*, one of the most popular values clarification programs on the market. Written for kindergarten to twelfth grade, *Quest* is used in over 20,000 schools nationwide.[1]

"What's wrong with the *Quest* program?" Is the question repeated over and over again, followed by: "Didn't Dr. Dobson write a chapter for the curriculum? It can't be all bad if Dr. Dobson endorses it, can it?"

To get the facts straight, Dr. Dobson of Focus on the Family wrote this letter of explanation for *Citizen* magazine:

> Let me begin by saying that Rick Little, developer of the *Quest* curriculum, and I are personal friends. I also wrote a chapter that was

included in the original *Quest* textbook back in 1979 — a chapter that remains there to this day. That is the extent of my personal involvement with the program.

. . . I wouldn't hesitate to point out that the *Quest* curriculum has a number of positive features. . . . Along with its good points, the program has what I feel are some serious problems. The authors of *Quest* have attempted in certain instances to incorporate the work of secular humanists into their curriculum, thus introducing elements clearly unacceptable to Christians. In other contexts they have prescribed group exercises and techniques closely resembling those employed in psychotherapy — a risky practice in the absence of professionally trained leadership. . . in the hands of an atheistic or anti-Christian teacher, *Quest* could become a vehicle for communicating some distinctly un-Christian values.[2]

Like Dr. Dobson, many parents are concerned about the content of this values clarification program and how it will affect their children.

Gene Haugen, a concerned parent, wanted to know how to respond to individuals who might be critical of the *Quest* program. He wrote to *Quest* international in Granville, Ohio, requesting information and received a polite letter thanking him for his interest and saying, "When concerns surface about any program, we find it's best to respect the concerns and encourage understanding by presenting facts rather than trying persuasive arguments."

The material included the "correct response" to any questions that might surface concerning the *Quest* program. When comparing what this material from the publisher says about *Quest* with the study done by respected experts and professors, however, there are some obvious discrepancies.

Let me take you on a quest for the truth in order to show

how the educational elite hide the facts in an effort to keep parents in the dark.

No Values Clarification?

According to Quest International *material:* "We do not have the students participating in values clarification activities. Rather we have identified the values to be imparted to children through classroom discussion and activities."[3]

On the other hand, Mr. Kirschenbaum, who was hired to co-author one of the *Quest* programs titled, *Skills for Living*, made this comment while speaking before the national convention of the Association for Supervision and Curriculum Development: "It has lots of values clarification in it . . . lots of self-talk."

What are we to think when Mr. Kirschenbaum's statement obviously contradicts the "correct response" provided by *Quest International?*

Not Humanistic?

According to Quest International *material:* "As I understand it, humanism is a belief that denies the existence of God and determines what is right and wrong by situation, that is situational ethics or humanistic values. *Quest* in no way supports these ideas. . . . We in no way intend for a child to become their own god or deny the existence of God."[4]

Mr. Kirschenbaum, however, had a different idea when he told the national convention of the Association for Supervision and Curriculum Development, "It's — I think you know — a really fine synthesis of alive humanistic education."

Doesn't humanism put man in the place of God? Isn't that why it's called human-ism? Once again the co-author of the program contradicts the propaganda put out by *Quest International.*

No Personality Testing?

According to Quest International *material:* "We in no way condone or suggest that a teacher take on the role of a therapist while implementing a *Quest* program. . . . *Quest* programs are not experimental, nor do they include psychological/psychiatric testing" [personality testing].[5]

According to Dr. Harold M. Voth, chief of staff of psychiatry/psychoanalysis at the Veterans Administration in Topeka, Kansas, "These exercises do amount to personality tests and some sections serve as guides for therapy."[6]

Dr. Joseph Adelson, professor of psychology at the University of Michigan, agrees that the *Quest* program constitutes personality testing. "In my view certain parts of the syllabus qualify as 'personality testing'."

He goes on to say:

> I am almost certain that most lawyers and most courts would hold this to be personality testing. Given the nature of these instruments, it seems to be quite clear that parental consent must be obtained, by provisions of the Hatch Amendment.[7]

The Hatch Amendment states that it is illegal for a child to undergo personality testing without the written permission of the child's parents.

Concerning *Quest*'s implementation of teachers as therapists, Dr. Voth has said, "Exposing the child to the broad issues introduced by the *Quest* exercises and orchestrated by teachers of unknown mental health and stability places the child in a position of great risk."

How are these teachers trained? William Kilpatrick, author of *Why Johnny Can't Tell Right From Wrong*, provides the answer to that question:

> Group leaders or "facilitators" of the *Quest* program are required to attend a three-day workshop that is basically a crash course in the techniques of client-centered therapy. The advice they receive is similar to the advice a fledgling

therapist might receive before meeting his first client.[8]

Aside from being dangerous, these kinds of "exercises" take precious time away from other subjects. Phyllis Schlafly makes the point when she says, "We send children to school to learn how to read and write, add and subtract, spell, and acquire some knowledge of our country, our government, and science. There is no place for group therapy in the public school classroom — or for psychological courses that are not academic."[9]

Reduces Drug Abuse?

According to Quest International *material:* Concerning the effectiveness of the *Quest* program in the area of acting as a deterrent to drug use as an anti-drug and alcohol program, *Quest International* material states: "There are no studies known to *Quest* which demonstrate that participation in *Quest* programs leads to subsequent use of drugs or illicit substances."[10]

Dr. Adelson, however, makes this startling conclusion: "I believe the school authorities ought to scrutinize closely the tacit substance of abuse. In the past, results for programs like this have been very mixed indeed. . . . Some of them actually increase drug use by stimulating curiosity."[11]

The Office of Educational Research and Improvement of the U.S. Department of Education in 1988 put out a booklet titled, *Drug Prevention Curricula: A Guide to Selection and Implementation.* On page 43, the department advised that selection of a program should be based upon a number of considerations. One of these is a "proven track record of success if purchased from a publisher."[12]

Quest does not have a proven track record. How do we know?

On December 23, 1989, Kathleen Honeycutt, a concerned citizen who was trying to evaluate the *Quest* program, wrote to *Quest International* requesting "actual documentation to substantiate their claim that their curriculum has been successful in reducing substance abuse." She received a package of information from Dr. Jerry Walker, Director of Evaluation for *Quest International*, containing summaries of 25 reports. None of them, however, provided documentation that the curriculum has been effective in reducing substance abuse among students.[13]

Professor William R. Coulson, a psychologist and one of the pioneers of *Quest*, now travels the country, apologizing to parents for his involvement in helping develop this course and warning of its dangers. In an effort to expose the flaws behind *Quest*, Professor Coulson reported:

> When I visited the Skills for Adolescence classroom in San Diego, there was a lot of talk about "I feel" statements. There is no way to explain but to say that students were practicing turning morality into reports of feelings.
>
> Although Skills of Adolescence is sold explicitly as drug education, there was no talk of drugs in the session I observed, and I was told that, by design, there would be none until the last three weeks of the course. Even then the focus would be on subjectivity and "decision making."[14]

So why bother? If you're not going to tell kids that drugs will destroy their minds, ruin their bodies, and eventually kill them, why go to all the trouble of instituting a "substance abuse" program?

Well, at least it helps the unemployment rate by forcing districts to hire a few new teachers to staff the classrooms.

Usurps Parental Authority?

According to Quest International material: Concerning undermining of parents and parental authority, *Quest International* states, "We believe that parents are the primary educators of their children. . . . Children are taught to be a better family member, not encouraged to evaluate or sit in judgment of the family or parents, nor do the programs usurp parental authority."

Concerned Women for America, in an August 1990 publication, had a different opinion of *Quest's Skills for Adolescence* program:

> *Skills for Adolescence* rather than serving as a source of reinforcement for the family, provokes the destruction of ties, dismissal of the family's accepted value system, and the perception that behavior, house rules, and discipline are negotiable.
>
> The student guide/textbook, *Changes: Becoming the Best You Can Be,* implies that conflict within the family is an expected variable in all homes, and no one, including the reader, is ever entirely at fault. In the introduction to the book, parents presumably excluded from this immunity, are referred to as "noisy prison wardens."[15]

What teenager wouldn't love to have his textbook reinforce what he already wants to tell his parents: "Mind your own business. I'll live my life the way I please!"

Such examples of brainwashing and indoctrination are not rare and uncommon exceptions. In fact, parents all over the country have reported similar cases of students being instructed not to tell parents what is being discussed in class. This has been documented by the United States Department of Education to have happened in Georgia, Maryland, Pennsylvania, Arizona, and Oregon.[16]

Phyllis Schlafly of Eagle Form reveals in a report titled, *Child Abuse in the Classroom,* that in a "values clarification" class in Oregon, third-grade kids were asked, "How many of you ever wanted to beat up your parents?"[17] In what was called a "health" class in Tucson, high school students were asked, "How many of you hate your parents?"[18]

A parent in Tucson who reviewed several similar courses that were being used in the local school reported that they "eroded the parent-child relationship by inserting a wedge of doubt, distrust, and disrespect."[19]

Such evidence would make any parent angry. When parents complain, however, they face opposition from all teacher, administrators, school board members — even the PTA!

The PTA's Guide to Extremism

Most of those in the educational elite have a lot of book sense but not enough common sense to realize when a program just will not work. Don't ever let anyone tell you as a parent, grandparent, uncle, aunt, or taxpayer that you are not qualified to speak on education because you do not have a bachelor of science or Ph.D.

One of the greatest preachers of our time, the late Vance Havner, said in his book, *Playing Marbles with Diamonds,* "You don't have to be included in *Who's Who* to know what's what."[20]

If you do decide to fight to have objectionable curriculum removed from your child's school, be prepared to be called an "extremist."

A concerned parent faxed to my office a brochure produced by The National Parent Teacher Association titled, *National PTA's Guide to EXTREMISM.* Whom do you think they are referring to as extremists?

The brochure had this to say: "Extremism is nothing new — it has always been a part of American life. In the past, extremism gave rise to the Salem witchcraft trials . . . the brutality of the Ku Klux Klan, the growth of the American Communist Party and the blacklisting of the 1950s."[21]

Are those the kinds of people attending PTA meetings? I thought PTA stood for Parent Teacher Association. Anyone who's ever been involved with the PTA knows it's usually the most concerned and dedicated parents who participate. Apparently, the National PTA thinks there are some dangerous "extremists" among their ranks! Talk about stereotyping in an effort to paint a certain image!

How do these extremists operate? "They [the extremists] try to polarize society, to intimidate their enemies and to rewrite history to serve their own uses. They try to depict a past that never really existed in an effort to reshape today and influence tomorrow."[22]

I get it. Only "extremists" are concerned about their children's future. The brochure goes on to say:

> Extremists oppose many efforts to reform, change, or improve what exists in America calling such efforts untrue to "traditional American values." A disturbing group of extremists tries to manipulate religious values to oppose or support positions. . . .[23]

Have you guessed whom they are talking about? It's those religious fanatics who believe in "traditional American values." You know, people like you and me!

Now here's the clincher: "Extremists demand total and unquestioning acceptance of their interpretations of faith and deny the possibility of other interpretations. . . Extremists try to stifle the free expression of all views opposed to their own."[24]

Liberals, however, are considered "progressive" — and never called "extremists" — no matter how forcefully they try to jam their radical agenda down conservative throats!

Who's Stifling Whom?

A case in point where the liberals stifled free expression occurred in February, 1993. Our friend Gary Bauer, president of the Family Research Council, had been booked to speak at a U.S. Coast Guard prayer breakfast for over six months. At the last moment the event was canceled. Why? Because Rep. Gerry E. Studds (D-Mass), who chairs the committee overseeing the Coast Guard got cold feet.

Gary Bauer said in the February 6, 1993, publication of the *Washington Post*, "I can't help but believe that since, in recent weeks, I have criticized the president's idea about changing military rules on how homosexuality is treated, that I have stepped on the lifestyle of the congressman."[25]

According to the article in the *Washington Post*, "Coast Guard spokesman, Captain Ernest Blanchard, said the breakfast was canceled because there were 'some concerns from members of the command that all religious affiliations were not represented.'"[26]

Nice excuse. Tell me, since when are the liberals interested in being sure that all religious beliefs — or beliefs in general — are respected? If they are so concerned about being fair, they should have let Gary speak.

It sounds to me that Congressman Studds and those responsible for the cancellation of Gary and the breakfast would fit the definition of an "extremist" as defined by their liberal friends at the PTA.

To quote the PTA again: "Extremists try to stifle the free expression of all views opposed to their own."

From what I have been told by his office, Gary's topic was going to be, "Family Life in the Military." Now there's a dangerous topic! No wonder Rep. Studds was scared!

While we're on the subject of stifling the opinions of others, let me give you an idea of what's happening on university campuses today. Dr. James Dobson, writes in a recent newsletter:

> I doubt if many parents realize just how antagonistic many of our states schools have become to anything that smacks of Christianity. There is simply no place for God in the system. "Diversity" is the new god which represents all world views and philosophies except one. The Christian perspective is not only excluded from the classroom, it is often ridiculed and undermined. The dominate philosophy in today's pub-

lic university is called relativism. . . .

There is, perhaps, less freedom of thought on today's secular campuses then any other place in society. A student or faculty member is simply not permitted to espouse ideas that are contrary to the approved "group think." This purity is enforced by what has been called "campus thought police," including faculty feminists, homosexual lesbian activists, leftists professors, animal rights proponents, minority activists, and the bilingual activists.[27]

In order to survive on America's college and university campuses, you better be "politically correct" or be prepared to be persecuted. There is no place in America where "free speech" is denied more than in the halls of higher learning.

A *Chicago Tribune* article titled, "Campus Speech Codes are on the Way to Extinction," notes that the University of Michigan established a "student guide to proper behavior" that discriminately lumps racist threats with such conducts as "failing to invite someone to a party because she is a lesbian."[28] Does that mean invitation lists must meet racial quotas before they are acceptable?

Imposing Lifestyles

The PTA brochure goes on to ridicule anyone who disagrees with their liberal agenda:

Extremists try to purge school and public libraries of books and materials that are objectionable to them. . . . Extremist groups are using censorship to change educational direction and to eliminate any reference to views that differ from their own.[29]

When a group of liberals, in late 1992, attempted to have the Bible removed from a public school library in St. Paul/

Minneapolis, no one screamed, "Censorship!" Instead, the non-existent, worn-out "separation of church and state" slogan was heralded throughout the liberal media.

I guess liberals do qualify as extremists — at least according to the PTA definition: "Extremists try to impose their beliefs, values, and lifestyles on everyone."

Remember our liberal friends who had the books, *Heather Has Two Mommies*, *Daddy's Roommate*, and *Gloria Goes to Gay Pride*, on the recommended reading list for first graders in New York? Was this not an attempt to impose a belief and lifestyle on young, innocent, and impressionable minds?

But it doesn't stop there. Pennsylvania State University advised its 10,000 incoming freshman in 1990 that they might be assigned a homosexual roommate and if so, they would not be permitted to object.[30] So much for freedom of choice.

According to the PTA brochure, "Extremists make irresponsible and unjust attacks on individuals and institutions and organizations that disagree with them. . . ."[31]

I wonder if the PTA would consider Ted Turner of Turner Broadcasting Network (TBN) an "extremist"? After all, Ted has called Christians "bozos"[32] and stated that Christianity is a "religion for losers." For some reason, I think the PTA might agree with Mr. Turner's statements. Besides they wouldn't want to stifle Ted's right to free speech.

Why does the liberal establishment despise those who call themselves Bible-believing Christians? The PTA brochure gives us a clue to their distorted thinking, when they say, "Extremists believe in absolutes."

I certainly hope so! The PTA would do well to be sure our kids are being taught absolutes such as, "You rob a bank and get caught, you are absolutely going to jail."

Deciding Who Can Vote

The opening paragraph of the brochure produced by the PTA reveals their true objective:

America's educational system is coming

under special attack by many extremists. They are trying to change education by controlling what students read and study and to shape our schools into a place for inculcating youth with their political, social, and religious views. Many extremists oppose public education. Some even wish to destroy the public school system and to replace it with a private system controlled by them.[33]

Now there's a great idea! As I recall, the most respected educational institutions in our nation were founded as private schools and funded by our Christian forefathers — not the federal government. Sure, I'd like to replace the public school system with one similar to the one my parents had the privilege of attending — where the Lord's Prayer was prayed every morning and students pledged allegiance to the American flag.

I guess that makes me an extremist.

Once they have ferreted out all the "extremists," the brochure tells how to keep them under control in this very prejudicial statement: "Be sure that only PTA members in good standing are allowed to vote at PTA meetings."[34]

Who decides whether are not you are in good standing? If you oppose them on something, does that put you in bad standing? Sounds like a pretty harsh statement for people who are supposedly so accepting of everyone and everything.

If you'd like to read this propaganda for yourself, write or call the PTA National Headquarters in Chicago, Illinois, and request your own copy of *National PTA'S Guide to EXTREMISM*. (See *Resources* for address.)

Censored Morality

In 1985, Paul Vitz conducted a federally funded study for the National Institute of Education on the content of textbooks in the public school. In his book, *Censorship: Evidence of Bias in our Children's Textbooks,* Vitz wrote, "Religion, traditional family values, and conservative political and economic positions have been reliably excluded from the children's text-books."[35]

Since the 1960s, America has experienced an ever increasing moral decline. What brought it about? The dramatic turn from the traditional standards of right and wrong to the belief in moral relativism. The result? An educational system that refuses to teach morality and even goes to great extremes to promote just the opposite — immorality.

Oxford's Mary Warnock presents the educational elitists dilemma: "You cannot teach morality yourself; and you cannot be committed to morality yourself without holding that some things are right and others wrong."[36]

Phyllis Schlafly has a name for this: "undirective education." She says that "adults have defaulted on the job and decided that they are *not* going to give children the wisdom and benefit of adult experience."[37]

What can we expect from kids who have been taught, "If it feels good do it"? What kind of behavior results from a generation who view themselves as "party animals" and think they were "born to be wild"? These statistics reveal the tragic consequences:

> • Arrests for rape among thirteen- and four-teen-year-old males have doubled in the last twenty years.
> • All violent crimes for male and female juveniles have increased by 55 percent.
> • More teenage boys die of gunshot wounds than all natural causes combined.
> • One in four adolescents is at risk of alcohol or drug addiction.
> • The rate of teenage suicide has tripled in thirty years.[38]

Is this what we want for future generations of American kids? If these are the results now, what will twenty or thirty more years of educational immorality training give us?

If our schools would promote a morally based value system founded on the belief that there is right and wrong and that wrong choices and decisions have consequences, the moral decline in our nation might be reversed.

Is there an answer?

Ronald T. Bowes, Director of Educational Planning for the Diocese of Pittsburgh, hits the nail on the head:

> We need more schools that teach the difference between right and wrong. We need more schools that stress moral and religious values. We need to give parents the ability to select schools that are an extension of their own principles and beliefs. To ignore these realities and fail to respond is to fail our children and destroy our future.[39]

Will we respond? Will we stop the educational abduction of America's children before it's too late? I hope so.

9

Robbed of Innocence: Sex Education's Hidden Agenda

The following paragraphs are just a few of many disturbing quotes from an eighth grade textbook titled, *Finding My Way*. See if you can determine what the authors, Audrey Palm Riker and Charles Riker, are trying to teach these students.

> During the past few years unmarried men and women have decided to live together without keeping it a secret. Give as many reasons as you can in favor of such an arrangement (p. 25).
>
> This is a time of great social change. The sex role revolution may cause the biggest upheaval of all. Old ways die slowly, many men and women will continue to act out traditional roles. They'll raise their children much the same as they were raised (p. 60).
>
> Some adults haven't kept up with changing lifestyles (p. 75).[1]

Such statements would lead a child whose parents enjoy a traditional marriage and choose to raise him with conventional values to feel abnormal and possibly part of a dysfunctional family.

Finding My Way is just one example of many such values clarification and sex education text books used in America's classrooms. Many of these books make the traditional family look like a thing of the past and portray traditional male-female roles as old-fashioned and out of touch with the times.

After getting kids to question — or even deny — the importance of the traditional family, *Finding My Way* goes on to give students a more open-minded approach to abortion by stating, "In spite of the Supreme Court's ruling, many people are against abortion for any reason."[2]

Since when does the Supreme Court's ruling on a decision make it morally acceptable? For many Americans, there is a moral law that rises above natural law.

After giving the "politically correct" opinion on abortion, the authors of *Finding My Way* go on to promote the advantages of teenage abortion and birth control with statements (or lies) like these:

> Studies show that sage legal abortions usually do not affect the female's health during future pregnancies. Most girls do not experience prolonged upset after they have an abortion. Much more common are temporary feelings of sadness, regret, guilt, and mild depression. These negative emotions are often balanced off by a great sense of relief (p. 159-160).
>
> It is unlikely that a female will become pregnant as long as she takes the pill as directed (p. 172).[3]

But if a girl does become pregnant or contract a sexually transmitted disease, the authors of *Finding My Way,* are more than happy to tell them where to go for help:

> Many city and county health departments
> offer free tests and treatment. So do many family
> planning clinics. Parents are not notified, no mat-
> ter how young the patient (p. 200).
>
> Most city, county, and private health clinics
> provide tests and treatment for VD. These free or
> low-cost services are kept confidential (p. 202).[4]

This type of advice teaches children not to turn to the people who love them most when they encounter very difficult situations. Instead, *Finding My Way,* encourages the child to seek the guidance of complete strangers while, at the same time, leading kids to believe that their parents are unreasonable, harsh, and out of touch with reality.

Chapter Four of *Finding My Way* deals with how parents tell their kids about sex and the inadequate job they do. In general, the text promotes a complete lack of respect for parents and their judgment when it comes to what is best for their child.

The book certainly strives to help a child find his or her way! Unfortunately, it's a dangerous and lonely path without a pre-determined set of values and with little or no parental assistance.

The Real Reason Behind Sex Education

At first glance, this next statement from *Finding My Way* sounds more mainstream: "Husbands and wives who don't have sex outside of marriage don't get VD."

We might assume the authors are trying to teach kids that chastity and monogamy are the best protections against vene-real disease — that is until we read their next statement: "This could be one reason why many parents are not fully prepared to teach about sexual diseases."[5]

What? Does this mean you have to be sexually active with numerous partners in order to qualify as a sex ed teacher? If so, then are students being instructed and influenced by the teachings of sexual perverts in their health classes?

This next quote from *Finding My Way* confirms our suspicions. Let me warn you, however, it is extremely graphic. But keep in mind, if you find this material offensive as an adult, how do you think exposure to this kind of trash affects your child? The authors write:

> Some forms of sexual behavior are considered very unusual. The person seeks a non-human object for sexual stimulation and release. Following are some examples: Bestiality refers to a sexual contact between a person and an animal. Bestiality is most likely to take place when a human sex partner is not available. Fetishism describes the behavior of a person who reacts sexually to a non-sexual body part or an article of clothing. The object, itself is called a fetish. A fetish could be a number of things including a foot, a lock of hair, a shoe, or a piece of under-clothing.[6]

Is this the type of material you want your child exposed to — and in a co-ed classroom? Why would any responsible adult, much less the authors of school textbooks — include such garbage for our children to read?

There can be only one reason: To desensitize and break down the natural and healthy, God-instilled walls of innocence, purity, and inhibition. Why else would the authors mention masturbation 31 times on two pages (pp. 206-207) of their "textbook"?

To further accomplish their purpose of breaking down traditional standards of decency and behavior, the authors encourage sexual deviancy with statements like these:

> Exposure to sexy materials is not likely to change the average adult's character or morals . . . . After looking at porn, many persons show more interest. They also talk more about sex. After a while, however, their attitudes toward porn tend

to go back to what they were in the first place. They may even end up a little more opposed to porn than they were originally . . . most persons quickly get their fill of pornography. After they have seen enough, they no longer feel pleasure or excitement (p. 89).

Children are not necessarily harmed or disturbed by child molesters (p. 241).

Sometimes sexual experiences help a person feel more secure and confident . . . (p. 249).[7]

Sounds to me like they are encouraging kids to build their confidence through "sexual experiences"!

You may be asking: Why doesn't someone do something to get this kind of trash out of our public schools?

Thomas and Karen Prischman, of Bismarck, North Dakota waged a long, tough battle to get the book, *Finding My Way,* out of their local school and won. The Prischmans knew this book was not "value-free" and that it actually enticed young people into a more liberal lifestyle.

Who will fight for the kids in your school district who are daily exposed to demeaning and pornographic material disguised as sex education? Will you?

Student Sex Survey

In Belulah, North Dakota, the Mercer County Women's Action and Resource Center developed a survey to be given to students in grades ninth through twelfth. According to the Women's Resource Center, the survey, "will give us information about students' sexual knowledge, decision-making and communications skills, importance of their values, and their attitudes toward abuse and sexual violence."[8]

Let me ask you: Is this kind of information any of their business? Will this survey improve the students' academic education? Of course not. That's not their objective at all.

The following are a few of the questions students were asked in the survey:[9]

• If a couple has sexual intercourse and uses no birth control, the woman might get pregnant:

    A. anytime during the month.

    B. only one week before menstruation begins.

    C. only during menstruation.

    D. only one week after menstruation begins.

    E. only two weeks after menstruation begins.

• When things you've done turn out poorly, how often do you take responsibility for your behavior and its consequences?

    A. Almost never

    B. Sometimes

    C. Half the time

    D. Usually

    E. Almost always

    F. Does not apply to me

[Notice that the moral answer is not even provided as an option.]

• Agree or disagree?

    A. Unmarried people should not have sexual intercourse.

    B. I have my own set of rules to guide my sexual behavior.

    C. Birth control is not very important.

    D. If you love someone, you should be willing to have sex with them.

    E. It is a good idea to live with somebody before marrying that person.

• To what extent would your friends be shocked if they thought you were having sexual intercourse?

• To what extent does guilt keep you from being more sexually active than you are?

    A. Not at all

    B. A little

    C. Medium amount

D. A large amount
E. A great deal
F. Does not apply

[Notice that in these two questions the option, "I do not believe in premarital sex" is not available, thus making the student feel weird or abnormal for being moral.]

• Having my current sex life, whatever it may be, I feel

_____.

Has your child ever been asked to complete such a questionnaire at school? If you're not sure, you may want to ask him or her. You may surprised to learn that sex surveys are often part of the high school curriculum and given without parental notification or permission. In fact, students are sometimes encouraged not to tell their parents about such questionnaires and their contents.

Rated "R"

In 1979, the U.S. Department of Health, Education, and Welfare produced a questionnaire for "health education" which included these questions:

> • How often do you normally masturbate (play with yourself sexually)?
> • How often do you normally engage in light petting (playing with a girl's breast)?
> • How often do you normally engage in heavy petting (playing with a girl's vagina and the area around it)?[10]

No wonder America's children are so preoccupied with sex. It's encouraged by our schools and promoted as normal behavior for a "healthy" teenager. Remember, these questions were developed in 1979. Can you imagine what they're asking kids today in the 1990s?

A textbook titled, *Changing Bodies, Changing Lives,* and widely used in schools and recommended by the School Library Journal, is liberally sprinkled with quotes from teens describing their sexual experiences in minute detail. As parents, you may find the following quotes from this book offensive, but keep in mind, your children are subjected to this kind of material on a daily basis in their school classrooms.

> Fred, a gay student, relates, "I was so excited the first time I had sex with a guy that I came just taking my pants off . . . ."
>
> Donna, a seventeen-year-old, describes her experience: "I was with this guy who said, 'Let me do something to you I think you'll really like.' And that was when he went down on me and started licking me. I was really kind of embarrassed . . . but it really, really felt good, and I relaxed and just got into it."

At regular intervals the authors remind their young readers, "There's no 'right' way or 'right' age to have life experiences and only you can decide what is right."[11]

Peter B. Dow, principal developer of a controversial fifth-grade federally funded program, "Man: A Course of Study" which challenges "the notion that there are 'eternal truths' [e.g., the Ten Commandments] that must be passed down from one generation to the next." What is the purpose of this challenge? Mr. Dow explains: "We are trying to break down the view that because your culture is good for you, it is not necessarily good for someone else."[12]

How is this done in the classroom? William Kilpatrick, author of *Why Johnny Can't Tell Right From Wrong,* illustrates:

> In these curriculums a lot of time and energy is spent exchanging opinions and exploring feelings, but practically no time is spent providing

moral guidance or forming character. The virtues are not explained or discussed, no models of good behavior are provided, no reason is given why a boy or girl should want to be good in the first place. In short, students are given nothing to live by or look up to. They come away with the impression that even the most basic values are matters of dispute. Morality, they are likely to infer, is something you talk about in class but not something you need to do anything about.[13]

The educational progression has worked. Students are first taught to question the authority of their parents, then stripped of their moral values, and presented with the idea that "if it feels good, do it."

If you think I'm overstating the case, let me quote directly from *The National Guidelines for Comprehensive Sexuality Education*. Published in 1991, by the Sex Information and Education Council of the U.S. (SIECUS), these "guidelines" give you an idea of how our government educators think. One recommendation is that children as young as five be told:

> . . . that "it feels good to touch parts of the body," that "some men and women are homosexuals, which means they will be attracted to . . . someone of the same gender," and that "adults kiss, hug, touch, and engage in other sexual behavior with one another to show caring and to share sexual pleasure."[14]

I will refrain from the sharing the details and language used in many "sex education" books to describe "sexual behavior." Suffice it to say that by the time a child enters fourth or fifth grade, he knows exactly what his parents are doing in bed at night, the benefits of mutual masturbation, and how to unroll condoms on bananas.

Dana Mack, a scholar at the Institute for American

Values in New York, explains the mindset of the "sexuality-education" experts:

> It seems no age is too young, no act too depraved to be excluded from the zealous reach of the "sexuality-education" experts. To these educators, the sooner and the more completely kids are divested of innocence in sexual matters, the less vulnerable they will be to repression, victimization, and disease.[15]

In our schools, it's okay to have extremely sexually explicit curriculum — to the point of being pornographic — but try to implement curriculum that promotes abstinence, and you're in for a fight!

Not Enough Sex?

In early 1993, a school board in Shreveport, Louisiana, who had implemented the abstinence curriculum, *Sex Respect* and *Facing Reality* was sued by a group of "concerned citizens." Why? They thought the value-based program was "promoting a religion."

For some reason they were offended by the *Sex Respect* curriculum, which encourages students to become emotionally mature and gives them good, solid, reasons for saving sex for marriage. To help them stick to their decisions, it teaches the importance of healthy dating and modesty. Accompanied by an extensive parents' manual, the program involves parents at every step, helping them understand the need for sexual abstinence for their teens.

Project Respect, the publishers of the curriculum, who went to the aid of the Shreveport School Board, said in a press release: "We were able to present clear documentation that abstinence is the healthiest lifestyle for our teens. Those who brought this suit presented no documents and only psycho-babble as to why promoting abstinence purportedly promotes 'a religion'."

Let me share with you a few highlights from the four day trial.

"Rabbi Michael told the court that it was an impossibility for the word 'spirit' to be used in any context other than a religious context. Yet he closed his testimony by stating, 'The spirit of these texts promote religion.'"[16] The parent supporters of the curriculum couldn't help but be amused by the rabbi's obvious contradiction of his own statement.

Project Respect pointed out in their press release:

> This is the same rabbi who objected during depositions to our statement: "Human reproduction has a higher meaning than animal reproduction." His objection was based on his certainty that his dog is indeed going to doggy heaven!
> Psychiatrist George Seiden argued that *Sex Respect*'s explanation about sexual arousal was not adequate. He drew his own charts for sexual arousal — one for males and a different one for females — and insisted that the seventh and eighth graders should be taught erotic explanations about multiple orgasms.[17]

So let me get this straight: If you promote abstinence, you are promoting a religion. So since we can't promote religion, we must be sure to be sexually explicit and graphic to the point that our kids are encouraged to have sex.

In April 1993, Judge Frank H. Thaxton III banned *Sex Respect* and *Facing Reality*. As a result, Caddo Parish School Board in Louisiana filed a request with Judge Thaxton asking that he lift his injunction against the two abstinence sex education curricula.

The Family Research Council reported this update in their May *Washington Watch* newsletter:

> Thaxton, after being bombarded with pro-test letters and facing an upcoming re-election

campaign, issued a statement "clarifying" his decision. Calling the suggestion that he had ruled against teaching abstinence "preposterous and outrageous," Thaxton stated that only specific words and phrases in the material were illegal. Without those phrases, the curriculum may be used.[18]

An appeal of the case is in progress.

In addition to the *Sex Respect* curriculum, there are other excellent programs. These are recommended by Focus on the Family:

— Spokane-based *Teen-Aid*
— Chicago's *Southwest Parents Committee*
— *Next Generation* in Maryland
— *Choices* in California
— *Respect Inc.* in Illinois.[19]

"Other curricula such as *Facing Reality*; *Me, My World, My Future*; *Reasonable Reasons to Wait*; *Sex, Love, & Choices*; *F.A.C.T.S*, etc., are all abstinence-themed programs to help kids make good sexual decisions."[20]

Elayne Bennett's *Best Friends Program*, a "mentoring" project that helps adolescents in Washington, DC, graduate from high school and remain abstinent. "In five years, not one female had become pregnant while in the *Best Friends Program.*"[21]

Where Are We Now?

Thomas Sowell, an economist and senior fellow at Hoover Institution and a nationally syndicated columnist, notes:

Does anyone ask himself why it takes years and years to teach school children so-called "sex education"? Obviously it does not. What takes years and years is to wear down the values they were taught at home and lead them toward wholly different attitudes and different conceptions of the world. Brainwashing takes time — and it takes time away from academic subjects.[22]

After years of sex education classes and values clarification instruction, what is the result? The reasoning behind such courses touted by the educational elite has always been: If we teach them about sex and remove the guilt associated with it, there will be fewer teenage pregnancies and sexually transmitted diseases.

So where are we now? Since the federal government began its major contraception program in 1970, "unwed pregnancies have increased 87 percent among fifteen to nineteen year olds."[23]

- In 1980, there were 27,700 unwed pregnant teens in the U.S. Ten years later, in 1990 — 46,800.[24]
- AIDS is the seventh leading cause of death among 15-24 year olds.[25]
- Three million teenagers are infected with STDs (Sexually Transmitted Diseases) every year.[26]
- In 1972, there were nearly 600,000 abortions performed. In 1990 — 1.6 million.[27]

Such evidence paints a clear picture of failure. Sex education classes and value-less instruction don't work. The tragic results are obvious.

By now, you would think the educational elite would have caught on and tried something else. Instead, they continue to view teenagers as mindless creatures with animalistic tendencies and drives that must be satisfied and can't be controlled. So, instead of teaching them abstinence and self-denial, the liberal elite prefer to give them the tools with which to gratify every sexual urge that comes along.

Why else would Jocelyn Elders recommend distributing condoms to school children from the fifth grade and up? Her low opinion of young people underscores her intentions.

The newspaper advertisement, "In Defense of a Little Virginity," produced by Focus on the Family, sums up the problem:

> Since 1970, the federal government has spent billions of our tax dollars to promote contraception and "safe sex." . . . Even if we spent another $50 billion to promote condom usage, most teenagers would still not use them consistently and properly. The nature of human beings and the passion of the act simply do not lend themselves to a disciplined response in young romantics.[28]

Patrick Buchanan, who also objects to the fallacies of the "safe sex" message, has made this profound statement on numerous occasions: "Abstinence works every time you use it. It has never failed."

Educators, however, refuse to make kids responsible for their sexual urges and seek to rob them of their innocence in the process. And if you get in their way — look out!

Banned by Planned Parenthood

Recently, in Grand Prairie, Texas, three fathers were arrested and charged with the class B misdemeanor of trespassing. What had these otherwise law-abiding citizens done to deserve this charge? Believe it or not, they were arrested while attending a public meeting held at the public high school in the school district where their children attend.

These three men were responding to an invitation by Grand Prairie High School to attend a public presentation geared toward teens. Not only were adults encouraged to be present, but students were told that they would receive extra credit for viewing the program. What the invitation didn't mention, however, was that the presentation, which was to be held in the high school auditorium on a school night, was actually sponsored by Planned Parenthood.

Aware of the deception, two of the fathers arrived early and from the school parking lot began passing out material on abstinence and informing parents that this was a Planned Parenthood presentation. The third father stood by watching. When parents realized the true nature of the program, many took their teens and went home.

Minutes before the start of the program, the fathers put their material in their car and went in to find a seat in the auditorium. After they had been sitting quietly in the back for several minutes, the vice principal of the high school approached the three men. He told them that he had custody and control of the building and would like for them to leave. The three fathers refused, stating that this was a public meeting and that their only intention was to sit and listen — which they continued to do.

I wonder how these fathers would have been treated if they had been promoting the homosexuality or abortion rights? They would probably have been welcomed as honored quests not only by Planned Parenthood but also by the school administration. Because they were encouraging abstinence, however, they faced the wrath of local officials.

Soon a police officer arrived and again the three fathers were told to leave. When they questioned why they were being forced to leave a public meeting, things got ugly. Before they knew it, the three men were arrested, taken downtown, booked for trespassing, and eventually allowed to post bond.

These three fathers are now awaiting trial. If convicted, they could spend 180 days in jail, and/or be fined $1,000. Fortunately, attorney Mark Troobnick of the American Center for Law and Justice is defending these three men. As a result of public opinion and fear of negative publicity, the superintendent for the school district has asked the district attorney to drop the case.

Although the outcome is still uncertain, this incident gives me reason to hope. I'm encouraged to know there are parents — especially fathers — who will take a stand against the garbage being thrown at America's children. At the same time, I'm glad to see that the hidden agenda of the educational elite and the sex educators has been exposed. Way to go, dads!

10

The Subtle Abduction: Why They Want Your Children

As the cornerstone of our society, the family has the greatest influence on children, especially in their early years.

Today's anti-Christian, pro-humanist movement, however, poses a serious threat to the moral and spiritual fabric of our society. This movement, with its relativistic and atheistic philosophies, strives to make obsolete and extinct the values, principles, and beliefs of the Judeo Christian family — the very same values, principles, and beliefs on which this great country was founded.

If those, who are a part of the New Age movement and the liberal left, (which includes the educational elite) are to accomplish their desired goals and plans, they must first break down and undermine the authority of the most influential institution of all time — the family. Just how does this humanist, relativistic, and politically correct movement of today plan to attack the family? Through the public educational system.

If you don't believe me, read what one of their own, John J. Dunphy, recently wrote in *Humanist Magazine:*

> I am convinced that the battle for human-kind's future must be waged and won in the public school classroom by teachers that correctly perceive their role as proselytizers of a new faith which will replace the rotting corpse of Christianity.[1]

Thomas Sowell, author of *Inside American Education,* asks,

> By what right do other people usurp the responsibilities of parents and use schools to carry on guerrilla warfare against the values that parents have taught their children?

Robert Morrison notes:

> The tie between parents and children is older, stronger, more intimate, and more demanding of government respect than any other attachment in society. Teachers were once rigorously taught that they acted merely in loco parentis — in the place of parents — when they had temporary charge of children. Society's appreciation of that fact created a bond of trust between parents and schools. That bond has been strained ... when the nation's largest public school system — New York City — moved to distribute condoms without parental consent or notice. Whether or not one agrees that teens should be given contraceptive devices, the action of Chancellor Joseph A. Fernandez shows how far American schools have come from that time when public educators

recognized that they acted only under limited and delegated authority.[2]

Why do we see such a blatant attempt by the educational establishment to undermine parental authority? Why do they seek to obtain exclusive and overwhelming power in deciding what they teach and promote to our children?

Brooks Alexander hit the nail on the head when he said:

> In the ideological contest for cultural supremacy, public education is the prime target; it influences the most people in the most pervasive way at the most impressionable age. No other social institution has anything close to the same potential for mass indoctrination.[3]

John Dunphy, a well-known humanist writer, makes it clear who will carry out the agenda of the educational elite:

> ... teachers must embody the same selfless dedication as the most rabid fundamentalist preachers, for they will be ministers of another sort, utilizing a classroom instead of a pulpit to convey humanist values in whatever subject they teach, regardless of the education level — preschool, day care, or large state university. The classroom must and will become an arena of conflict between the old and the new — the rotting corpse of Christianity, together with all its adjacent evils and misery, and the new faith of humanism. Humanism will emerge triumphant. It must if the family of humankind is to survive.

Marilyn Ferguson admits in her book, *The Aquarian Conspiracy,* that of the many "Aquarian Conspirators" she surveyed, "more were involved in education than in any other single category of work. They were teachers, administrators, policy makers, and educational psychologists."[4]

A New Consciousness

Through today's educational system, the ancient Judeo Christian values and ideals are being replaced with a new consciousness. A consciousness that focuses on the deity of each individual no matter how great or small. To prove my point listen to what Gloria Steinem, a well-known feminist and humanist stated, "By the year 2000 we will, I hope, raise our children to believe in human potential, not God."[5]

The New Age movement proclaims that the insane and insincere doctrine that man is full of sin and needs to be cleansed with the blood of Jesus Christ, lest he be condemned to hell, is false. Such a belief would only be taught by individuals who want to control and manipulate the lives and actions of others.

Gloria Steinem again proves my point, when in an interview with *Saturday Education* in 1973, she made the following statement:

> The point is to enlarge personal choice, to produce for each child the fullest possible range of human experience without negating or limiting the choices already made by the adults closest to her or him.

Parent, let me ask you: Who is the adult closest to your child or children? You are, the mother and father. In short, Gloria Steinem is saying it is imperative that we teach children that their beliefs and values do not have to be the beliefs and values of their parents. Each child should know that they have the right to choose what they believe. The end goal, of course, is to undermine parental authority so it would be easier to influence that child in humanistic, atheistic, and relativistic doctrine.

What small child would not naturally choose to follow and accept a philosophy that encourages them to make their own decisions and never uses the word no! After all, there is no such thing as right and wrong in this new age. Besides, the pundits say, to tell a child no only has a negative psychological effect on his early childhood development; thus, potentially creating an emotional scar he would carry with him the rest of his life.

Thomas Sowell, notes how educators use classroom curriculum to accomplish their goals:

> Central to this questioning of authority is a questioning of the role of the central authority in the child's life — parents. Alternative ways of constructing individual values, independently of parental values, are recurring themes of curriculum materials on the most disparate subjects, from sex to death.[6]

Our children are being educated in the belief that "decisions are not to be made by relying on traditional values passed on by parents or the surrounding society. Instead, those values are themselves to be questioned and compared with the values and behavior of other individuals or other societies. This is to be done in a neutral or 'nonjudgmental' manner, which does not seek to determine a 'right' or 'wrong' way, but rather to find out what feels best to the particular individuals. This general approach has been called values clarification" (which we discussed earlier).

Why is such a blatant attempt being made to undermine the authority and influence that parents have on their children? Thomas Sowell provides the answer:

> Parents are the greatest obstacle to any brainwashing of children, and it is precisely the parents' values which are to be displaced. If parents

cannot be gotten out of the picture or at least moved to the periphery, the whole brainwashing operation is jeopardized. Not only will individual parents counter what the brainwashers say; parents as a group can bring pressure to bear against the various psychological conditioning programs, and in some places get them forced out of the schools.[7]

When does this brainwashing start?

T.A. for Tots

Thomas Sowell is his book, *Inside American Education* states, "The undermining of parental authority can begin quite early." Sowell describes how an author in the "transactional analysis" school of psychology, which is often simply called "T.A." has developed a book designed for children in preschool through third grade, entitled *T.A. for Tots.*

Sowell writes,

One of the pictures has a caption: "Hey, this little girl is crying" and a butterfly on the side of the picture says: "Oh! Oh! Looks like she got a spanking." The picture of the next page shows the same girl spanking her doll and saying "No, No!" The caption reads: "Ah ha! Now she is being bossy and spanking her doll. Who taught her to do that?" The butterfly in the corner says: "Could it have been daddy and mommy?" The recurring theme of the book is that little boys and girls are born as little princes and princesses. At first, in infancy, they are treated that way and feel that way. But parents end up turning these princes and princesses into frogs, in their own minds, by constantly criticizing and punishing them.[8]

Sowell reports that nearly a quarter of a million copies of this book for young children has been sold within the past four years.

A quote directly from the book, *T.A. for Tots*, states:

> Sometimes things happen you don't like. You have the right to be angry without being afraid of being punished. You have the right to tell mommy and daddy what you don't like about what they are doing.[9]

The not so subtle message is that mommy and daddy are being bossy when they punish you, and you have the right to tell them that you don't like it and it makes you angry. Children are being taught that they are little adults who have the right to be treated as they see fit. Indeed, we are to respect our children as human beings who have been entrusted to us by God for the purpose of raising and nourishing. But to think that a child should have the right to tell his parents, "I am mad at you because you punished me for lying, and I think you're being bossy," is absurd.

Since when was punishment supposed to be a fun and enjoyable experience? Many kids are in trouble today because they do not have the appropriate respect for rules and authority nor the understanding that there is a price or punishment to be paid for wrong choices.

Dangling the Forbidden Fruit

The educational system is using the same tactics on America's children used thousands of years ago. In the Garden of Eden, Satan deceived Eve into accepting his humanistic, atheistic, and relativistic lie. Satan appeared to Eve and convincingly asked, "Did God really say you must not eat from the tree that is in the middle of the garden?" If I were to paraphrase this scene into today's language it would sound like this:

> *Satan:* Did God really say you can't eat from this tree?
>
> *Eve:* Well yes, God has told us that we could eat fruit from any tree in the garden that we want, except the tree that is in the middle of the garden. He even told us not to touch it or we would die.
>
> *Satan:* Oh come on, give me a break, you won't die. The only reason He told you not to eat the fruit on this tree is because He knows that if you do, you will be just like Him. You see, if you eat the fruit on this tree, you will have an esoteric experience. You will have all knowledge; you will know everything. He also knows that if you eat the fruit on this tree, you will be just like Him — God. You will be able to decide what is right and what is wrong. You will be able to create your own reality and control your own destiny. You will be your own salvation.

Today's educational system, along with help from the media, dangles the forbidden fruit of the New Age movement in front of today's kids, telling them of the joys and benefits of partaking.

When Satan appeared to Eve in the Garden of Eden, in the form of a serpent, he did not have the advantage of appealing to Eve's sin nature. It is much easier for Satan to deceive and devour the Adams and Eves of today because we *do* have a sin nature. Our sin nature naturally wants to accept and follow the lies of Satan represented in the New Age movement.

That's why we must have the Word of God hidden in our hearts — so we won't sin against God. I cannot say enough about the importance of reading and memorizing Scripture with your child or children, at the youngest possible age. Proverbs 22:6 says, "Train up a child in the way he should go and when he is old he will not depart from it."

Kids today know more than we give them credit for. That's why we must be busy instilling our values into our children, at the youngest possible age — especially in this day and time.

As Dan Quayle said on February 19, 1993, at the Conservative Political Action Conference, "Teach your kids values or someone else will."

Engrave your principles and values on the heart of your children in a way that has promised to never return void. "So shall my word be that goeth forth out of my mouth; it shall not return unto me void" (Isa. 55:11).

The Rockefellers, John Dewey, and the NEA

It is very clear through our brief look into education that a concerted effect is being made to limit the power and influence that parents have in the process of instilling chosen values and beliefs into their children. The facts are clear. The educational system and liberal elites are determined to undermine parental respect and authority to insure their own influence and power in the indoctrination process. That's why humanist John Dunphy believes this is a must if the family of humankind is to survive.

According to reporter Robin Wilson of *The Chronicle of Higher Education,* the National Education Association (NEA) "has attacked parents' moves to gain more control, saying that they have gone overboard and that teachers cannot be effective under veto power."[10] What do they mean? That they can't be as effective at indoctrinating your children if you interfere.

The NEA does not want parents, who are also taxpayers, to have any control in the educational system. That's like wishing that the stockholders, who actually own the company, had no say about the operation of the business. The NEA tells parents, "You can pay the bills and have the financial responsibility of everything, but don't give us any advice; and you can't have any power to call the shots."

How in the world did we get to this point in America?

The NEA has it roots in the General Education Board established by John D. Rockefeller in 1902. To ensure control of this tax-exempt organization, Mr. Rockefeller put his assistant, Frederick T. Gates, in charge as chairman.[11] Gates revealed the Rockefeller philosophy on education in the board's *Occasional Letter, No. 1.*

> In our dreams we have limitless resources and the people yield themselves with perfect docility to our molding hands. The present educational conventions fade from our minds, unharmed by tradition, we work our good will upon a grateful and responsive rural folk.[12]

In other words, because parents are too stupid to train their children properly, we'll take America's children and mold them into a mindset that will benefit our socialistic goals.

Gates' dream of limitless resources for the General Education Board was not mere fantasy. In fact, Gary Kah, author of *En Route to Global Occupation,* explains how large sums of money were contributed to the General Education Board by the Rockefellers.

> Between 1902 and 1907, John Sr. would give a total of $43 million to the GEB. And from 1917 to 1919 he and his son John D. Jr., gave a combined total of $200 million to the GEB, the Rockefeller Foundation, and the Laura Spelman Rockefeller Memorial. The total amount of Rockefeller funds given to influence education from 1902 to 1930, in today's money would be equivalent to more than $2 billion. This is an incredible sum of money going to promote globalism and socialism within education.[13]

Many such socialistic, humanistic, and globalistic philosophies were also promoted by the "father of modern education," John Dewey, who wrote:

> There is no God and no soul. Hence, there are no needs for the props of traditional religion. With dogma and creed excluded, then immutable (unchangeable) truth is also dead and buried. There is no room for fixed, natural law, or permanent moral absolutes.[14]

George Washington, who could not tell a lie, is called the father of our country; and John Dewey, a liar, is called the father of modern education.

John Dewey, a committed humanist who promoted the humanistic lie of Satan, has had a major influence on many of today's educators. How much influence?

> Today, 20 percent of all American school superintendents and 40 percent of all teacher college heads have advanced degrees from Columbia where Dewey spent many years as the department head.[15]

The National Education Association also received a large amount of funds from the Rockefeller and Carnegie Foundations and today is "the largest union in America (with two million members and an operating budget of $135 million) and the most influential and powerful force in the education establishment."[16]

By 1934, the NEA had adopted John Dewey's philosophy of "humanism, socialism, and globalism, and incorporated it into the classroom."[17]

In addition, John Dewey's personal ties to the Rockefeller family "went back a long way as he taught four of the five Rockefeller brothers, including David and Nelson."[18]

In an effort to control the minds of American children,

the Rockefellers "not only used their money to seize control of America's centers of teacher training, they also spent millions of dollars rewriting history books and creating textbooks that undermined patriotism and free enterprise."[19] These books promoted Marxist propaganda to the extent that the California legislature refused to appropriate money for them.

Rene Wormser, the council for the Reece Committee, which investigated foundation control over teacher training schools, concluded:

> It is difficult to believe that the Rockefeller Foundation and the National Educational Association could have supported these textbooks. But the fact is that the Rockefellers financed them and the NEA promoted them very widely.[20]

It is also interesting to note that in the mid 1930s, John Dewey visited "Russia for a time to help organize the Marxist educational system there."[21]

These documented events make it clear why the NEA is really not so interested in representing teachers, as much as they are interested in promoting their own political and social agenda. A quick look at the history of the NEA proves this statement to be true. Despite the fact that "more than half of the NEA membership voted for Ronald Reagan both in 1980 and 1984,"[22] the NEA itself endorsed Jimmy Carter. "Two-thirds of teachers polled by the NEA in 1985-86 classified their political philosophy as conservative or leaning toward conservative."[23]

Why then do many of America's teachers and educators, who claim to be conservative, continue to support and pay dues to the National Education Association? Most of the teachers I know personally have traditional values, are family-oriented, and raising their kids to discern right from wrong. Why haven't they rebelled against the liberal, socialistic agenda of the NEA? Does the NEA have such economic, political, and moral power over the teachers of America that they are afraid to take a stand for the values they believe are right? I'd like to know.

Senator Hoagland

During a radio talk show with then State Senator Peter Hoagland of Nebraska and the pastor of a local fundamental Christian school that had been closed by the state for lack of accreditation, Sen. Hoagland made these outlandish remarks:

> What we are most interested in, of course, are the children themselves. I don't think any of us in the legislature have any quarrel with the right of the reverend or the members of his flock to practice their religion, but we don't think that they should be entitled to impose decisions or religious philosophies on their children, which could seriously undermine those children's ability to deal in this complicated world when they grow up.[24]

Today Peter Hoagland is a United States Congressmen for the second district of Nebraska.

A United States Congressmen should be a servant of and for the people, protecting their rights as listed in the Bill of Rights. Telling parents they do not have the right to indoctrinate their children in their faith, does not sound like someone interested in protecting the rights of his constituents. It is chilling to think the personal agenda and beliefs of a few people in strategic places can potentially affect the freedom of many.

In March, 1992, I was preaching in the evening service at the First Evangelical Free Church in Lincoln, Nebraska. In my sermon I mentioned this quote by Congressmen Hoagland, as well as the fact that he was up for re-election in November. The next Tuesday morning back in St. Paul, I received a phone call from Hoagland's press secretary. "So Mr. Howse, we understand that you were in our state this past weekend and were saying some things about the congressman that were not true. We would greatly appreciate it if you would cease and desist."

"Well", I said, "it is true that I was in Nebraska this past weekend and, yes, I quoted Mr. Hoagland, but you know as well as I do that I quoted him accurately."

After a few minutes of discussing whether or not Congressman Hoagland had made this statement or not, I informed the press secretary that I had in my possession a tape of the television interview on which Hoagland had made this statement. I sent it off to him, and we never heard from the congressman or his office ever again. Hoagland won re-election in November of 1992, but barely.

When is Religion Not a Religion?

The Supreme Court of the United States has ruled that prayer and Bible reading are illegal in public schools because Judeo Christian beliefs constitute the teaching of religion.

Yet, two U.S. Supreme Court decisions (*Torcaso* v. *Watkins* 367 US 488 [1961] and *U.S.* v. *Seeger* 380 US 163 [1964]), expressly acknowledge humanism's religious nature.[25] Instead of being banned as a religion from the public school system, however, humanism is promoted and incorporated more earnestly than ever. As a result, the religion of humanism and relativism oozes from today's educational system.

Programs paid for with federal dollars, are purposely used to advance certain doctrine on school children that is totally contrary to the beliefs of most parents. Not only is this wrong morally, but it is contradictory to the parents' constitutional rights based on the parent-child relationship.

The United States Supreme Court, in the case of *Edwards* v. *Aquillard* (1987) (482 U.S. 578, 583-584) decided:

Families entrust schools with the education of their children, but condition their trust on the understanding that the classroom will not purposely be used to advance religious views that may conflict with the private beliefs of the student and his or her family.

11

Impressions:
Breeding Ground for the
Occult

What are the first impressions your young elementary child receives during his or her very important and formative years in education? For children whose schools use the *Impressions* reading curriculum, they get a full dose of witchcraft and the occult right off the bat!

Let me share some excerpts from some of the *Impressions* series published by Harcourt, Brace, and Jovanovich (HBJ) and written for kindergarten through sixth grade.[1]

> A real witch is easily the most dangerous of all the living creatures on earth. That's a pretty horrifying thought. More horrifying still is that real witches don't even look like witches. They disguise themselves as nice, ordinary ladies. (From *Cross the Golden River,* project book, page 42.)

In *Cross the Golden River*, project book, page 80, project #1 titled, *The Sorcerer's Apprentice*, the teacher tells the children:

> • The sorcerers are in need of new apprentices. Form small groups of sorcerers to decide how to go about finding your new assistants.
> • Conduct a group interview session in which there are several applicants and several sorcerers interviewing.
> • Can you think of a situation in which a sorcerer might have to cast one of these spells?
> • How do you think the sorcerer would say the spell?

From the *Impressions* sixth grade *Teachers Resource Book*, page 58, comes more occult training: "Have the students discuss the belief in fortune telling. What aids does someone use, for example: tea leaves, palm reading, tarot cards, crystal balls."

In a play titled, "The Beamy Brown Eye," from the *Teachers Anthology 3* for *Cross the Golden River*, pages 50-52, one child is forced to play the part of a witch. Here's a sample of the script:

> Narrator: The witch beat on a tombstone with the two long thigh bones.
> Witch: Has anyone down there seen my beamy glass eye? My beamy brown eye?
> Narrator: The witch used her rusty key to open the graves. The ghost and skeletons arose from the ground.

The story, "Zini and the Witches," by Ruth Manning-Sanders, also from the *Teachers Anthology 3*, pages 16-17, would put fear into the heart and mind of any child:

And he looked in another dark place and saw nothing. And then he lifted a curtain to look in a third dark place, and he saw it — it isn't easy to say what he saw. There were bodies and bones, and all sorts of horrors.

So then Zini knew his wife was a witch. . . . Zini tried to run away, but they rushed at him and dragged him into the cave. They tied his hands behind his back and stood him before the Chief.

"You deserve to die for this," said the Chief. "But I will spare your life on one condition. Bring me the hearts of your mother and sister and you shall live. Not only shall you live, but you shall become one of us. We will turn you into a mighty witch, and you shall help your wife to work evil."

Then he ordered the creatures to free Zini's arms, and told him to go home.

"Tomorrow night I shall expect you again, with your offering of hearts," he said. "If you do not come, I shall see to it that your wife skins you alive."

That's enough to give any normal child nightmares for the rest of his young life! The authors of these stories obviously don't have any idea how such suggestions of violence — especially against a mother — affect children.

Rosemary Chiaferi of the Child Guidance Center believes this kind of material is "potentially disturbing to children" since it presents youngsters with the threat of "loss, physical injury, cruelty to animals, kidnapping, and nightmares."[2]

In the innocent sounding story, "The Little Mermaid," found in the fifth grade *Teachers Anthology*, page 24, a witch cuts off the mermaid's tongue. Then the witch scratches her breast, lets her black blood drip into the cauldron, and makes a potion from it.

From the sixth grade *Teachers Anthology*, page 63, the

story, "Sir Gawain and the Green Knight," details a description of cutting off a head from a bleeding, headless body. Yet the head still talks.

In the fifth grade reading book, page 11, children are forced to read the story, "Thread the Needle, Beauty and the Beast":

> "We have just the thing for you," roared the giants. "All day long we have been digging a pit just for you. And so that you won't be bored, we have stuck sharp knives and razors into the sides of it so here goes."
>
> They flung the prince into the pit. By the time the prince reached the bottom, he was cut into a thousand pieces. When the prince remained silent, the giants disappeared.

Now there's a pleasant image for ten-year-olds to ponder on their way to recess! But that was nothing compared to what they had read the year before in fourth grade:

> The boots kicked and clomped, twisted, turned, and in mad, frantic frustration banged me this way and that against the fence, until I was bruised and crying from the pain, holding on for life and in despair that there would be no end to the contest until my arms were torn from my body and I was carried off a horrible broken and bleeding stump to greet my mother and father without even the arms to hug them before we were brought to our end. (From the *Fourth Grade Teachers Anthology*, page 21.)

And you thought your kids were reading stories about George Washington and selections from *Little Women* and *Little House on the Prairie*.

"Oh, no. Kids today are too sophisticated for such drivel,"

the educators explain when parents question the use of such graphic violence in reading texts. "Kids want blood and guts and gore, so that's what we intend to give them — like it or not!"

In addition to the occultic and gruesome content, the undermining of parental authority is also a common theme in *Impressions*. In the *Teachers Anthology* for fourth grade, page 78, we read: "School was a sort of punishment. Parents always want to punish their children, and school is their most natural way of punishing us."

So parents are made to appear as ogres who enjoy seeing their children suffer, so they send them to horrible places like school!

Secret Ammunition

The *Impressions* series troubles many parents — and for good reason. One scholarly survey found these percentages of occurrence in the reading material:

- "violence/degradation and death" in 27 percent;
- "negativity and despair," in 27 percent;
- "witchcraft/magic/animism," in 22 percent;
- "bizarre/unusual illustrations," in 38 percent.

In addition, "sorcery and witchcraft appeared in 52 percent of all the reading selections."[3]

In many states, the *Impressions* series has become so controversial that Harcourt, Brace, and Jovanovich, the publisher, has published a defense kit for superintendents, school boards, and administrators to use in dealing with the outcry from parents.

Janet Spalding, director of sales support services for HBJ, includes a letter in the three-ring binder accompanying the "defense kit" that contains this underlined warning: *Please use the information in this notebook with discretion.*[4]

In Fairbanks, Alaska, Cheri Hensley, a parent who was visiting Jan McNelly, director of curriculum for the Fairbanks School District, had the opportunity to view the binder for a few minutes. As soon as Ms. McNelly saw her reading this "secret" material, she ordered a secretary to take it.

"They snatched it right out of my hands," Hensley said.

Jan McNelly said, "This is not for public viewing."[5]

When Mrs. Hensley later returned to the district office with her attorney, she was permitted to see the binder but could not locate some of the material she had previously read. Then she noticed that the kit did not have numbered pages, making it difficult to detect whether pages were removed.[6]

At a later time, Jan Spalding, the curriculum director, was asked, "What is a defense kit?" Assuming this person to be a supporter of the *Impressions* series, Ms. Spalding replied, "It is a distillation and condensation of the material in the binder. It's easier to use, plus it does not contain some of the sensitive information in the binder."[7]

When asked, "What do you mean by sensitive information?" Ms. Spalding explained, "Sensitive information like from other districts that have fought parents and have developed rebuttals and techniques for defending themselves against parents. It's very important that the binders do not fall into the hands of the opposition because they are our ammunition."[8]

When do they use this "ammunition?" At school board meetings, superintendents and educators, in an effort to ward off parental criticism of *Impressions,* have been known to read directly from the "defense kit."

Why are educators so defensive when it comes to the *Impressions* series?

Beyond Imagination

Clinical Psychologist Scott Voss, a member of the Professional Occult Response Team, published a review of the *Impressions* series. Alarmed by his findings, he concluded:

After reviewing this curriculum, a number of serious concerns were raised in our minds about its literary value and actual purpose.... We object to a great deal of the curriculum's content which centers on witchcraft and occult-related themes. We believe that many of the stories in curriculum encourage youngsters to seek out and develop a relationship with negative supernatural powers. . . .

Repeated story themes of ghosts, demons, witches, and the use of spells desensitizes youngsters to what is in reality a very frightening part of life. The use of repeated chanting, as encouraged in this literary curriculum, has long been known for its hypnotic or trance-like effect and this technique is clearly a part of present-day occult rituals. . . .

In our professional opinion, this curriculum content and the techniques it espouses cultivate a susceptibility in youngsters to illustrations in this curriculum are exactly of the type we have personally observed in working with victims of ritualistic abuse and occult involvement. . . .

The methods that are used as well as the story content is strikingly similar to very destructive occult practices and because of this, we would consider this portion of the curriculum to be potentially dangerous for youngsters.[9]

Sergeant Paul Ruffolo of the Naperville, California, Police Department, and a member of the Professional Response Team, is also Occult Crime Investigator and Consultant as well as the lecturer for the Office of International Criminal Justice. The other five members of the team are also specialists and experts in the occult and ritualistic behavior. Their comments about the *Impressions* material underscores the hidden dangers of such teaching.

Police Officer Thomas C. Jensen, of San Jose, California, notes that exposure to occult practices "does affect children — I see how it affects them when they get older in criminal activity."[10] What kind of criminal behavior has this seasoned officer witnessed? "Vandalism, especially in schools, cruelty to animals, assault and batteries against parents and teachers, possession of dangerous weapons, drugs, sex, and suicide attempts."[11]

Jensen writes:

> I have found that among teenage involvement in the occult, there is an early phase that displays high levels of stress, anxiety, fear, feelings of inadequacy, alienation, anger, and ultimately building to fits of rage and revenge. The *Impression* series will tend to promote this kind of behavior even at a much younger and more impressionable age![12]

Jensen goes on to say that "the *Impressions* series will serve only to create a disruptive atmosphere in the classroom over a period of time as it promotes fear and violence through its writings."

Fred Eisenbraum, an Occult Crime Investigator for the Rapid City Police Department, said exercises from *Impressions* mirror those in books that teach beginning witchcraft. At a hearing on *Impressions* before the Douglas School Board in Box Elder, South Dakota in December of 1990, Eisenbraum said, "We are beyond imagination here. These are real rituals that are detailed in these books."[13]

Children Killing Children

My ministry office has received stacks of information on *Impressions* from concerned parents all over the country. The following quotes were compiled by a group of Illinois parents, who sent the *Impressions* material to several occult experts for their opinions on the curriculum. Let me share their startling statements with you.

Sergeant Tony Pearsall of the Vallejo Police Department and Youth Services and Occult Research has this to say about *Impressions*. "It crosses the line from simply 'exposing' to actually 'propagating' a religion."

Officer Greg Doyle of the Upland Police Department: "School children at that age level do not have the ability to discern between fact and fiction. Children will tend to pick up on the unreality and incorporate it into the way they deal with life."

Thomas C. Jensen of the San Jose police department, who has been researching and investigating the occult since 1985, responded with these written words:

> The *Impressions* series is a breeding ground for the occult, involving ritual activity such as chants, spells, lighting candles in a circle, and fortune telling. This activity is all consistent with witchcraft or the Wicca religion. On page 55 of the second grade teacher anthology, it reads, "Where ever there is hunger and sickness it is because the spirits of the dead are unhappy."[14]

"This thinking is common in the occult," Jensen says. Protection from the spirits for health and safety is often "accomplished through animal sacrifices."

Several recent news accounts have involved the shocking stories of children killing other children. A ten-year-old boy in New York state apparently murdered a four-year-old child by crushing his skull with a rock. Neighbors said the accused boy was known to be violent and abuse animals, having killed another neighbor's cat.

Police Officer Jensen notes that the content of the *Impressions* series is similar to that found in the lyrics of songs by heavy metal groups like Motley Crue, Slayer, Venom, Wasp, Dead Kennedys, and Iron Maiden.

In a Dead Kennedys' album, they sing:

God told me to skin you alive.
I kill children. I love to see them die.
I kill children and make their mamas cry.
Crush them under my car, I want to hear them scream.
Feed them poisoned candy to spoil their Halloween.[15]

Linda Rawson, a child abuse specialist for several school districts, said that what concerned her about the *Impressions* series is "the thought implied that there is no one in this world you can trust."

Michael Rattray, a private practitioner has said, "The material ... sets up in them a value system which is not absolute but relative to their own desires."

I could continue to share with you page after page of disheartening information, but the evidence is clear: This curriculum definitely leaves an impression! After all, everything kids do, see, or hear, makes an impression on them. What type of impression is being left on the young and impressionable minds of the children subjected to ritualistic, occult violence, and witchcraft day after day in their classrooms?

Even if the *Impressions* literary series is not being used in your school district, it's likely that your children are regularly being exposed to dangerous occult practices in their curriculums. If you don't believe me, ask to see the reading books being used in your child's classroom. It could be making a lasting impression that will affect his or her life for years to come.

Keeping Kids from Evil

Thomas Jensen notes: "As parents and teachers, we are role models for our children. We need to build self-esteem, not tear it down with negative thinking, violence, and fear. We need to encourage our children."[16]

What's the best way to do that? With the Word of God.

Proverbs 3:3 tells us to "write the laws and commandments of God upon thine heart and bind them about thy neck." Give your child wisdom through the Word of God, and this wisdom will keep them from evil. How do I know? Because Proverbs 2:10-12 tells us the benefits of wisdom.

> When wisdom entereth into thine heart, and knowledge is pleasant unto thy soul, Discretion shall preserve thee, understanding shall keep thee, To deliver thee from the way of evil men, from men that speak perverse things.

The saying is true: "Input, output what goes in must come out." What's being put into the mind of your child?

12

Hollywood and the Media: War on the Traditional Family

The battleground to preserve the traditional family and the values of our Judeo Christian faith goes beyond the classroom and reaches into our homes. Each and every night the troops of the liberal media set out to advance their humanistic and relativistic beliefs and agenda to a nationwide audience.

Their goals are many, but among them is to convey to America that the traditional family of yesterday, as portrayed in "Leave it to Beaver," is a thing of the past. A family with a father like Ward Cleaver, a mother like June, and two clean-cut, well-mannered sons like Wally and the Beaver, no longer exists. In fact, what we would consider a normal family is often portrayed as a group of right wing, fundamental, religious misfits who are out of touch with the times. Hollywood wants us to believe that the family next door is now more like the Simpsons or the television family of Roseanne Barr.

"The Simpsons," the prime-time cartoon, aired on the Fox Network revolves around Bart Simpson, a foul-mouthed boy of about ten years who calls his father by his first name and has absolutely no respect for authority. In spite of his youth, Bart has already been cheating his way through school, working for the Mafia, looking at pornography, gambling, and taking part in a host of other reprobate activities.

"Roseanne," is presently one of the top-rated television shows in America. I find it hard to believe the same audience that watched "The Cosby Show" for years and kept it number one in the ratings has now switched to the obnoxious Roseanne for its entertainment.

The perverted, shallow-minded show, "Married with Children," also has a large viewing audience. In fact, even their re-runs, which are in syndication, out-pace other shows running opposite them.

Is it any wonder that the traditional family is declining in numbers? While the liberal media and Hollywood are busy portraying the "Simpsons," "Married with Children," and "Roseanne" as the normal American family, most Americans are eagerly jumping to accept this portrayal as accurate. After all, if these television families are not normal, then my family is not normal; herein lies the lie and trap of the Hollywood left.

If the normal, respected American family was portrayed by today's writers and producers as the Clevers from "Leave it to Beaver," then, American's would strive to be like the Clevers. Thus, the opposite is also true.

Americans are led to believe that the normal American family consists of children and adults who are disrespectful to their elders, make a practice of lying, use situational ethics to solve problems, cheat on their mates, indulge in pre-marital sex, deny the existence of God, and live by the belief that we must eat, drink, and be merry, for tomorrow we die. As a result, many families who gain their values from television, accept this portrayal as the norm and make it the standard by which to live.

The Cultural Civil War

Charlton Heston said it well when he commented, "The moving image is the most powerful tool or weapon to change and shape the way people feel about the world and themselves. The printed word is almost primitive — like hammer and stone — measured against film and television. Its influence doesn't compare."[1]

According to the Index of Leading Cultural Indicator, March, 1993, "Americans are watching nearly two hours more television per day than they did three decades ago. Today, the average American watches nearly 50 hours a week of television — ten hours more than the average work week."[2]

My question is: Where do they find 50 hours of television worth watching?

In commenting on these facts, William Bennett writes, "Perhaps more important than the quantity of television is the quality. Today, there is more brutal violence and explicit sex on television than ever before. It has been estimated that by the time the average child reaches age eighteen, he will have witnessed more than 15,000 murders on television or in the movies."[3]

So how does this all this violence affect children? Researchers have found that "heavy exposure to televised violence is one of the causes of aggressive behavior, crime, and violence in society."[4]

That only applied to other peoples' kids, you say.

Don't fool yourself. Television violence "affects youngsters of all ages, of both genders, at all socioeconomic levels and all levels of intelligence . . . . It cannot be denied or explained away."[5]

Gary Bauer, author of *Children at Risk,* writes, "Hollywood is a powerful weapon in our cultural civil war. Its values, in the guise of entertainment, are promoted in our living rooms and on thousands of movie screens. Our children are particularly influenced by the value messages they receive that ridicule traditional beliefs and undercut commitment to family and faith."[6]

Dr. James Dobson, author and radio host of "Focus on the Family," has said,

> It was not Dan Quayle's [Murphy Brown] comment that outraged the media. It was the blatant endorsement of traditional morality — of the institutions of marriage and parenthood — of this being one nation under God — of the distinction between right and wrong — and of the Judeo Christian system of values . . . . And make no mistake about it: Those "politically incorrect" concepts emanating from the Christian faith are despised by people in the media. They would destroy the family and its moral foundation in a heartbeat if given the chance. Indeed, they work on that project 365 days a year — as evident in the "Murphy Brown" program and other trash served up to us as entertainment."[7]

"But that's what the public wants!" the television industry retorts. "If they don't like it, they have the option of switching to another channel."

Does the American public want this kind of trash thrown into their living rooms night after night? John H. Court, in the book, *Rebirth of America,* writes: "Violence and obscenity fill the media, despite the fact that this material does not reflect the choice of the average adult."[8]

Planned Parenthood conducted a study and found there are 30,000 sexual references on prime-time television each year. Out of those sexual references, thirteen to one are in reference to sex outside of marriage.[9]

In the November, 1992, episode of the sitcom "Seinfeld," the entire program revolved around the subject of masturbation. The three men and one women cast had a bet to see who could go the longest without masturbating. Before the end of the show, all four individuals had given in to the temptation.

This was the entire story line.

In a discussion with an assistant to one of the writers, I was told that they received more negative letters on this episode than any other previously aired show of "Seinfeld." In spite of this, the program was re-aired in the spring and billed as "the most controversial Seinfeld ever"! Apparently, the producers didn't care what their viewers or the public thought, and turned around and threw their garbage back in our faces.

William Bennett defines the problem when he writes that we live in a time "in which certain ideas prevail, certain messages are sent. And these messages act to encourage or discourage particular attitudes and behaviors. It makes an enormous difference, for example, whether children get messages from television telling them that honesty is the best policy, and to honor their father and mothers — or messages telling them that adultery is the norm, and that the breakup of a family is an expected thing. Likewise, if schools, churches, elected officials, community institutions, and neighborhoods are reinforcing parents' efforts, it makes their jobs easier. If the institutions of society work at cross-purposes (as they often have over the last two decades), the job is harder."[10]

Gary Bauer has said, "By and large, television programming reflects the anti-family side of America's cultural civil war."[11]

Michael Medved, author of *America* v. *Hollywood*, writes:

> People who try to maintain some kind of standard are sometimes laughed at, because it's so easy to do it the other way. It's a culture of scandal. The problem I have with it is the portrayal of America as a freak show. Every institution is corrupt. The family is finished. The church is disgusting. Our military is no good. (Remember, we weren't going to be able to beat the formidable Iraqi Republican Guard.) The news shows, the so-called reality shows, the talk shows — "Mothers of Lesbian Nuns Who Murder Their

Lovers" — all reinforce one another.

The one thing you never hear about in the popular culture is normal life. People loving each other, raising their children, paying taxes, going to church, having a decent existence. But whenever I say this, the response is always. "Do you want to go back to the days of 'Ozzie and Harriet'?" I'm not suggesting that. But it would be nice to see more wholesome entertainment occasionally.[12]

Well, I'm suggesting it! I think it would be a great idea. In the meantime, we can watch the "oldies" on increasingly popular cable channels like Nickelodeon and the Family Channel.

What Really Sells?

In the August 1992 issue of *US Magazine*, the cover story was "SEX in Entertainment: How Far Can It Go?" The headline for the lead story was, "Welcome to the New Sexual Revolution — the One Waged by the Entertainment Industry." The article goes on to say, "Mix up some sex and violence, throw in a psycho killer, and you've got yourself a hit."

But is that really what sells?

Many of the record-breaking movies over the past few years have revolved around families and their experiences. For instance, *Home Alone* grossed over five hundred million dollars, not to mention the millions of dollars that were made through home video sales, making it one of the most profitable movies in history.

As Michael Medved so accurately points out,

Look at the big surprise hits of 1992. *Sister Act*, the most profitable movie of the year in terms of return on investment, had the most affectionate attitude toward the Roman Catholic Church of any movie in a decade. *Beethoven* . . . was about a shaggy St. Bernard and a cuddly family. It's about as politically incorrect as it could be: that it's better for the mother to take care of her kids full-time rather than work outside the home. But it made $80 million — and they didn't even have to pay the dog. *The Mighty Ducks,* about a peewee hockey team, was a huge hit. *Aladdin,* the new Disney picture, is like a license to print money.[13]

In 1991, G and PG movies did three times the business on average as rated R films, yet 61 percent of all films are rated R.[14]

If these movies are so popular and make so much money, why does Hollywood continue to produce much more trash than treasure? The answer is that writers and executives are more eager to use their positions to promote their philosophies and agenda.

Samuel Goldwyn once said, "If you want to send a message, go see Western Union, don't see me." Today, most directors and producers would reverse that statement. Michael Medved has said, "A lot of the major studios are increasingly resembling telegraph offices."

It is obvious that the Hollywood writers and producers have not done their home work. According to the Census Bureau, 70 percent of the kids in this country live in two-parent families. The traditional family in America does exist, whether or not the liberal left in Hollywood wants to admit it.

And no matter how hard they try, the traditional family will not become extinct. As long as you and I continue to instill into our children the values of hearth and home based on the traditional lifestyle, there will be a traditional family with traditional values, generation after generation. Yes, our numbers are getting smaller, but we are still alive and well, and don't let them win by making you think otherwise.

Open Season on Christians

In *Alien 3,* a disgusting little monster movie, the inhabitants of a penal colony in outer space are drooling, vicious, rapists, and murderers who say: "We're all fundamentalist Christians."

Michael Medved asks: "What's the point? Why throw that in unless you're trying to score on ideological point against your Christian opponents?"[15]

In *Cape Fear,* Robert Denaro, portrays a deranged psycho killer who has a big tattoo of a cross on his back. He is seen throughout the movie reading his Bible and quoting Scripture, of course out of context. At one point in the movie, the character that Robert Denaro plays, says to the screen wife of Nick Nolte before attempting to rape her, "Are you ready to be born again, one hour with me and you will be speaking in tongues."

Rush Limbaugh writes,

> One of the things I've been perplexed about throughout my career, and especially recently, is the viciousness the left expresses toward funda-mentalist Christians — the whole notion that they're fascists, they're Nazi-like. I've never un-derstood this. Because as I've looked at it, its the people on the left who are trying to silence people they don't agree with.[16]

A good example of the liberal left attempting to silence the conservative right wing would be "Columbia Studios, which allowed its facilities to be used for NarcAnon, Alcohol-ics Anonymous, the Gay and Lesbian Alliance Against Defa-mation, formally banned a group from its property because they were studying the Bible after hours. Now we all know about separation of church and state. But nothing in the Constitution mandates separation of church and studio."[17]

Another example of Hollywood anti-family and anti-Christian attitude is "the main subplot of Fox Network's 'Key West' which features the town's gay mayor as the hero who is hounded by right-wing fanatics. Another character in the 'Key West' program is described as 'a no-nonsense prostitute' who is seen making love to a paraplegic's husband as the handicapped woman watches. The executive producer, David Beaird, said, 'We will very definitely make Dan Quayle hate us.' And a few million others, I hope!"[18]

Who are the few million that David Beaird wants to offend to the point that they would hate the Fox Network? Most likely fundamental right-wing conservative Christians.

Rush Limbaugh again makes the point when he writes:

> What amazes me about these people is that any attempt to maintain standards, which by anyone's definition are decent, right, wholesome, is looked upon with such anger and as a threat . . . . Whenever religion is mentioned, these people go ballistic. I think that's what we're really facing, a bunch of people who want no limits, moral or otherwise, on their behavior.
>
> "If God does exist, they know they're in trouble. The idea that someone might believe in a God who judges the work, who judges our behavior, is seen as a horrible, intolerable threat. This also goes to the controversy over the National Endowment for the Arts. Those in the creative community always say, "We're not interested in values that are nihilistic, and messages that attack traditional standards. They will praise work, regardless of its merit."[19]

Let me encourage you with this next statement by John Damoose, vice president of advertising for the Chrysler Corporation. "We are seriously questioning whether we want to continue advertising on prime time, we're questioning whether those dollars aren't being frittered away. It's apparent that with the decline in ratings, the networks have chosen to increase the content of sex and violence, which we absolutely will not support."[20]

You may want to write to Mr. Damoose, and thank him

for his bold stand for morality and traditional values. You can send your letter to: Mr. John Damoose, 1200 Chrysler Dr., Highland Park, MI 48288, or phone (313) 956-5741.

A Course in Deception

ABC's news program, "20/20," featured Marianne Williamson, one of the main promoters of humanism and relativism in Hollywood. After the segment ended, Barbara Walters, who is usually quick to question anyone's motive, had only words of praise for Williamson. Even *Time* magazine called her the "Mother Teresa for the '90s" and "the guru of the movement in Hollywood."[21]

Marianne Williamson teaches from the text, *A Course in Miracles,* a 1,200 page book written by a Jewish psychologist, Helen Schucman. The book "teaches spiritual self-betterment through exercises to clarify the subject's perception of reality."[22] Marianne has said, "The course was my personal path out of hell."[23]

According to *Time* magazine, "Every Saturday morning at St. Thomas Episcopal Church in West Hollywood, Marianne Williamson steps to the pulpit before a packed house. But she is no ordinary minister: the church has been rented and the message is decidedly New Age non-denominational."24

Williamson, who dresses in expensive designer clothing, gives three lectures a week, charging $7 per person, and, according to the television show "Hardcopy," makes $30,000 a month.

In addition, Williamson has produced more than fifty cassettes summarizing the course in miracles and written a book titled, *Return to Love,* her review of *A Course in Miracles.* Williamson has said, "We're experiencing a rebirth of early sixties thinking."[25]

Christianity Today, makes this conclusion: "The Course, as it is often called, includes a workbook with 365 lessons; about 1,500 groups in the U.S. meet each week to study The Course." *A Course in Miracles* was supposedly "channeled" by a voice who identified himself as Jesus Christ.

One of Marianne Williamson's most ardent supporters is Oprah Winfrey. When Williamson appeared on Oprah's talk show to discuss, *A Course in Miracles,* Oprah enjoyed her so much, she had Ms. Williamson return to the show and bought a copy of *Return to Love* for everyone in the audience.

Marianne Williamson has said, "Love in your mind produces love in your life. This is the meaning of heaven. Fear in your mind produces fear in your life. This is the meaning of hell."

Why do the broadcasting elite and talk show hosts, who at every opportunity eagerly condemn evangelical pastors and televangelists, praise and promote Marianne Williamson? Because she's singing their song: I'm okay; you're okay; let's love everybody; just don't mention the word "sin".

Michael Jackson — Divinely Inspired?

Who can figure out Michael Jackson, one of the most popular entertainers of all time? Dave Hunt explains what may be at the source of Michael Jackson's eccentric personality:

> A favorite even among some deluded Christians, Jackson believes he is a prophet sent forth as a messenger to the children of the world. He claims, "I worry about the children, all my children all over the world, I live for them . . . I was sent forth for the world, for the children, but have mercy, for I've been bleeding a long time now."
>
> Michael Jackson attributes his creative ability to the "force within" and reveals that his songs are given to him by way of revelation through "dreams" after being assembled in another realm.
>
> He says, "The whole thing is strange, you hear the words, everything is right there in front of your face, and you say to yourself, 'I'm sorry, I just didn't write this.' It's there already. I feel that somewhere, someplace, it's all been done, and I'm the courier bringing it into the world."

The Word of God reveals three different sources of dreams: natural (Eccles. 5:3); divine (Matt. 1:20); and evil (Jer. 23:32; 27:9; Zech. 10:2). Therefore the Lord instructs us to test those who claim revelation as a "dreamer of dreams" (Deut. 13:1-5) and "if they speak not according to this Word it is because there is no light in them" (Isa. 8:20).[26]

Remember the 1986 song, *We are the World,* sung by a host of stars and the theme song for "Live Aid," which was viewed by 1.5 billion people? For many, this song, written by Michael Jackson and Lionel Richie, is the anthem of the New Age movement.

Michael Jackson said the song was "divinely inspired." Who was the divine influence? Let me give you a clue.

One line from the song says, "Just as Jesus turned the stones into bread." If you consult your Bible, you will find that Satan tempted Jesus to turn the stones into bread, but Jesus, refused and responded by saying, "Man can not live by bread alone."

Harry Belafonte, a well-known entertainer, admitted that the purpose of the song, *We Are the World* was not so much about feeding the starving people of Ethiopia, as it was "to create a sense of globalism and unity and oneness in the children."

Many of these so-called "benefits" are designed to create a platform on which the liberals and New Agers of Hollywood can promote their beliefs and agenda. Harry Belafonte himself admitted to participating for those very reasons.

But what about Michael Jackson? What is his agenda?

One of the newer attractions at Disneyland is a short, 3-D film called *Captain EO* starring Michael Jackson as a spaceship captain sent to transform an evil planet. The film is blatantly New Age, with Jackson frequently flashing a T-shirt emblazoned with a glowing rainbow. An overall theme is that you cease to be evil when you discover the beauty inside of you, and the ending song contains such phrases as: "We are here to change the world, we're bringing brighter days, You're one of us, and you're just another part of me." George Lucas, who originated the *Star Wars* saga, was the creative force behind *Captain EO*.[27]

The line that goes, "You're one of us, and you're just another part of me," is describing the New Age doctrine of monism. Monism is the belief that all is one; everything is interrelated. New Agers believe we are separate in substance, but in essence we are one.

Teenage Stupid Ninja Turtles

The New Age influence knows no bounds and has even found its way into Saturday morning cartoons. You only have to watch a few children's programs before subtle references to magic, witchcraft, and hypnosis become obvious.

Cultural expert, Terry Mattingly, in a column titled, "My Daughter Loves to Watch Teenage Mutant Ninja Turtles," asks the question: How important is it to monitor your child's TV viewing? In discussing the dangerous New Age doctrine espoused by the Turtles, Mattingly notes:

> The cartoon "Ninja" faith is based on the ancient Eastern religious practice called Kung Pau, which includes hypnosis. Ninjas are assassins who train their minds, bodies, and spirits as weapons. When their faith is perfect, Ninjas are said to gain the eyes of their god and see into the future.[28]

To prove this point, read a portion of the actual words spoken by two of the Turtles:

> *Leonardo:* Now, everybody close your eyes and concentrate, concentrate hard.
>
> *Splinter:* I am proud of you my sons. Tonight you have learned the final and greatest truth of the Ninja. That unlimited mastery comes not of the body but of the mind. Together there is nothing your four minds cannot accomplish. Help each other draw upon one another, and always remember the true Force that binds you. The same as that which brought me here tonight. That which I gladly return with my final words. I love you all, my sons.

So what is this force that binds the Turtles together? Is the same force mentioned in the *Star Wars* movies? If so, where does this force get its power? I can only guess.

Know Any Bozos?

Media mogul, Ted Turner, founder of Turner Broadcasting and CNN, when speaking before a group of broadcasters, told them: "Your delegates to the United Nations are not as important as the people in this room. We are the ones that determine what the people's attitudes are. It's in our hands."[29]

While that statement tells us something about Ted, this next one, quoted in the *Denver Post*, shows where he's really coming from: "If America is to survive through the year 2000, it must elect a New Age president."

Then Ted Turner goes beyond the media and politics and exposes his anti-Christian bigotry unashamedly, when, in a speech to Hollywood Radio and Television Society, he encouraged businessmen to "stand-up, get off your knees, and go back to work instead of spending all your time praying."[30]

Turner, who pushes his ten "voluntary initiatives" — a humanistic alternative to the biblical Ten Commandments — has said: "We're living with outmoded rules. The rules we're living under are the Ten Commandments, and I bet nobody here even pays much attention to 'em, because they are too old.

When Moses went up on the mountain, there were no nuclear weapons, there was no poverty. Today, the commandments wouldn't go over. Nobody around likes to be commanded. Commandments are out."[31]

Turner went on to tell the members of the National Newspaper Association that the biblical Ten Commandments do not relate to current global problems, such as overpopulation and the arms race. Turner, who has called Christians "bozos", considers Christianity "a religion for losers."

At least we don't have to wonder what Ted thinks about us. But it does make me question how he — like Hollywood — intends to use his powerful broadcasting empire to promote his anti-Christian, New Age agenda.

Let's face it, we can't expect those who hold beliefs diametrically opposed to the Bible to produce programming that will benefit and encourage moral, family life. That's why we, as Christians, must be wise in our television viewing. Parents, especially, need to be careful what they permit their children to watch.

In a day and time when almost everyone has or can afford a relatively inexpensive VCR, we should use this tool to tape, purchase, or rent quality programming that will promote family values and encourage Christian character.

As one father said recently, "We don't watch network television. It's too risky. I rent videos so I can preview them before I show them to my kids. Even with G and PG, you never know what you're going to find. More times than I can name, we've rented what we thought was a decent movie and had to turn it off in the middle because they repeatedly took the Lord's name in vain."

Would you invite a foul-mouthed drunk into your house to visit with your children? Then why permit actors and actresses to pollute your godly home and assault your family with their obscene, blasphemous language and behavior?

Take a stand. Set limits. And don't back down. If you can't, get rid of the TV and VCR. That's a sure way to come out the winner in Hollywood's war on the family.

13

A New World Coming: Like It or Not!

Those who follow the metaphysical, self-made religion, of the New Age — and teach it to America's children — are striving to bring about a new world. Under the guise of "education" and "entertainment," they perpetrate their belief that the world's philosophical, religious, and political structures must be changed.

Expecting to usher in the Age of Aquarius or the age of new beginnings through a conscious revolution, they force their thinking on America's youth. By developing a new consciousness, they hope to focus on a oneness with God, all mankind, the earth, and the entire universe. Once this new focus and consciousness is realized, they can chart the path and destiny of this new world.

Such is the thinking of the deceived. I believe many New Agers are sincerely searching for the Truth. When they realize the emptiness and bondage that accompany all false religions, I pray they will eventually find eternal life in Jesus Christ. Some, however, will continue to deny the Son of God, and the

Creator's plan for mankind. "They perish because they love the truth and refuse to be saved" (2 Thess. 2:9-12). According to the Bible, the world God created moves according to the predestined plan and purpose of God's will. (See Eph. 1:11.)

Ultimately, there will be a new world order, but the fanatics of the New Age will not be able to take credit for it. Satan, the father of lies and deception, is the ultimate conspirator behind this new world order.

Satan, however, is using certain individuals to play a part in helping create an acceptance of the great changes ahead. Yet, regardless of how hard they try, the New Agers cannot bring about a new world through a conscious revolution.

Why not? Because God, who created the world, is still in control. Centuries ago, He revealed to the apostle John that a one-world government, one-world economical structure, and one-world religion will occur ruled by the Antichrist who is under the control of Satan.

> He [the Antichrist] was given power to make war against the saints and to conquer them. And he was given authority over every tribe, language, and nation. All inhabitants of the earth will worship the beast — all whose names have not been written in the book of life belonging to the Lamb that was slain from the creation of the world (Rev. 13:7-8).

One World — Like it or Not!

Scripture is clear that a one-world government will occur, and it will be lead by the Antichrist. "For God has put it into their hearts to accomplish his purpose by agreeing to give the beast their power to rule, until God's words are fulfilled" (Rev. 17:17).

Many of today's leaders are making statements to the effect that a one-world government will and must occur. A Harvard professor has stated, "A one-world government is in the making, whether we like it or not."[1] The late Prime Minister of India, Indira Ghandi, was quoted as saying, "We can survive in peace and good will only by viewing the human race as one."[2]

Science fiction author and founder of the Humanist Association, Isaac Asimov, predicts that "a government-run computer bank will record in its vitals every bit of ascertainable information about every individual in the United States (or in the world, if we are ever intelligent enough to work out a world government)." He also said, "The wave of the future: a planetary society in which all humans have a stake."

President Jimmy Carter's message to outer space, which was attached to Voyager I and II space crafts and intended for intelligent life in space read: "The voyager spacecraft was constructed by the U.S. of America . . . a community of 240 million human begins among the more than four billion who inhabit the planet Earth . . . still divided into nation states, but rapidly becoming a single global civilization."[3] The cover story of *USA Today*, June 2, 1988, began by saying, "The world is really becoming a global village."

Futurist magazine, reporting on a conference on computer networking stated: "There are many ways in which . . . peace organizations, churches, and student groups, can, along with businesses and governments, use such global scale tools, to help all of us function as citizens of the emerging global village."[4]

James Warburg, of Germany's Banking House of Warburg, stated as he stood before the U.S. Senate on February 17, 1950: "We shall have world government whether or not we like it. The only question is whether world government will be achieved by conquest or consent."[5]

United Nations?

There is growing evidence that the world is beginning to accept the possibility of a one-world leader. During the winter of 1989, the Berlin Wall came down with a resounding ring of freedom. Since then, communism has been all but completely defeated around the world.

In May, 1990, the much publicized visit of President Gorbachev to the United States was proof that the U.S. and the USSR were moving toward a new relationship. Now with the free, former Soviet Union and its new leader, Boris Yeltsen, it is clear that the world is moving closer to a climate that is less parochial and, therefore, more susceptible to the notion of a one world government.

Robert Muller, who served the United Nations for 35 years and was before he retired, assistant secretary general in charge of coordinating the work of 32 agencies and world programs of the United Nations, reportedly stated that the uniting of Europe set for 1992 was a "step towards a world community . . . we need a world or cosmic spirituality."

In a book entitled, *July 20, 2019, Life in the 21st Century,* the author closes with these words: "I cannot see the United Nations as anything more than a transition stage, toward a time when the very concept of 'nation' is meaningless."[6]

Gary Kah has said, "The UN represents a limited form of world government. Had the CFR, (Council on Foreign Relations, which worked with the state department to establish the UN) tried to bring the U.S. into a world government all at once, the effort would have failed. The American people would have reacted full force against such an attempt. The immediate purpose of the UN was, therefore, merely to warm Americans up to the idea of global government. It was all apart of the conditioning."[7]

John Whitehead wrote in *The End of Man:* "The American people will rebel if they consciously realize what is happening. However, if this trend toward control continues to move slowly, there will most likely be little resistance."[8]

This one-world government will ultimately crown a one-world leader, an event many prominent individuals await with anticipation.

Stephen Holley and Macol Hash wrote in their book, *Looking for That Blessed Hope:*

The late Belgian premier P. H. Spaak was quoted in *LaSeur Newspaper* as suggesting that "what we need is a person, someone of the highest order or great experience, of great authority, of wide influence, of great energy ... either a civilian or a military man, no matter what his nationality, who will cut all the red tape ... wake up all the people and galvanize all governments into action. Let him come QUICKLY!"[9]

Henry Spanks, a prominent leader of the Common Market, has stated, "We do not want another committee. We have too many already. What we want is a man of sufficient stature to hold the allegiance of the people, and lift us out of the economic morass into which we are sinking. Send us such a man, and be he God or Devil, we will receive him."[10]

666 — Just a Number?

The one world government will form a worldwide economic system controlled by the Antichrist. No one will be able to buy or sell unless he has the mark, or the number of the Antichrist.

David Spangler, a New Age author, in the book, *Love Is*, used the number 666 several times in various pictures. The numerals are thought to be a message to "the masters of the hierarchy," of which the Lord Maitreya is a part. The message is a plea for the "masters" to come and help usher in the New World.

Some New Agers believe that each time the numeral 666 is used, either in speech or in a picture, a message is sent to intelligent life in outer space, asking them to come to earth and assist in the bringing about of a New World.

Christians believe that the number 666 is the mark of the beast as stated in Revelation 13:16-18:

And he causeth all, both small and great, rich and poor, free and enslaved, to receive a mark in their right hand, or in their foreheads, And that no man might buy or sell, except he that had the mark, or the name of the beast, or the number of his name. Here is wisdom. Let him that hath understanding count the number of the beast; for it is the number of a man; and his number is six hundred three score and six.

As we look at the meaning of these verses, we understand that the mark of the beast, or Antichrist, is a number that will be used for the purpose of buying and selling. According to Revelation 13:17, no one will be able to buy or sell without this number.

Today's technology can place an invisible number on a person's hand or forehead that can easily be read by running a specially designed scanner over the area on which the number is printed. This means of buying and selling may not be as far off as some think. In fact, the United States government has funded development of a solution that will protect the skin from the effects of the laser scanners.[11]

When Christians think of the number 666, we immediately associate it with the mark of the beast or with occult graffiti. The number 666, however, can simply be the number that follows 665. Yet, on the other hand, this number is being used by some for the purpose of increasing acceptance of what many consider evil.

Rick McGough in his book, *One Minute Till Midnight,* lists some of the following examples of the use of 666:

1. When the Suez Canal was reopened after an eight year closure, a flotilla of ships, headed by a warship carrying Anwar Sadat, sailed through the canal. The numbers 666 were painted on the prow of the president's ship.

2. The overseas telephone operator's number from Israel is 666.

3. Some new credit cards in the United

States are now being assigned the prefix 666.

    4. Some large chain stores around the world have all their transactions prefixed with 666.

    5. Federal government Medicaid service employees division uses the number 666.

    6. The World Bank code number is 666.

    7. Australia's national bank cards have 666 on them.[12]

Is all this coincidence? Or is there an orchestrated effort to prepare the world, through positive exposure and influence, to readily accept the Antichrist and his one-world government?

Smart Cards

With today's current technology, a one world economical system is possible like never before. Dave Burnham, wrote in, *The Rise of the Computer State*, "Within the next decade or so, these computers will spin dozens of new communication networks across the face of America. One massive communication network, for example will substantially change the way we pay for almost everything we buy."

Burnham goes on to state:

> The increased use of EFT, as a substitute for cash means more transactions could be monitored through electronic networks, as the speed of various computerized banking system increases the potential for instantaneously learning the activities of an individual grows.[13]

According to *Futurist* magazine, "Pocket change, credit cards, and most forms of identification soon will be replaced by 'smart cards' — plastic cards that contain a microprocessor and a memory. Smart cards are the first step toward the old sci-fi notion of a totally computerized society without money or paper records."[14]

According to Frost & Sullivan, Inc., a New York based market research firm, "the technology necessary for widespread use of smart cards already exists. U.S. banks and retailers, however, are reluctant to make large investments in smart-card readers and other hardware until a standard format has been agreed upon. . . . Smart cards are already routinely used in Paris to make telephone calls, and one-third of all Japanese bank cards could be smart cards by the early 1990s. Smart cards may also replace travelers' checks, medical records of all sorts, tickets, licenses, college records, and inventory controls."[15]

The *Jerusalem Post*, January 6, 1990, wrote that the Israeli banking system is moving toward a cashless society based on a super card.

A Global Religion

In addition to a one-world government and economic system, we can expect to see a global religion that embraces all known religions — and any new ones man may dream up. True Christians, who know their Bible and have read the Book of Revelation, will refuse to take part in this worldwide deception. We need to be on guard because the groundwork has already been laid.

In 1988, many world religious and political leaders attended a Global Survival Conference in Oxford, England. On January 15-19, 1990, the same conference was held in Moscow, where "more than 100 participants from 83 countries call for a 'new planetary perspective' involving a 'new spiritual and ethical basis for human activities on earth.' In his address to the Forum, Mikhail Gorbachev called it 'a major step in the ecological consciousness of humanity.' "[16]

Albert Gore, who was then a U.S. Senator, spoke to the Moscow delegates and declared: "I do not see how the environmental problem can be solved without reference to spiritual values found in every faith."[17] In the end, the final "Moscow Declaration" called for "a global council of spiritual leaders" and the "creation of an interfaith prayer."

Global Forum's newsletter, *Shared Vision,* declared: "We need to remember our natural origins and re-learn how to love and respect nature. The love of our eternal parents, Earth Mother and Sky Father, is all embracing."[18]

At a 1990 World Peace Day, Pope John Paul addressed a prayer gathering of Christians, Muslims, Jews, Buddhists, and others. The Pope told the conference participants that their efforts were unleashing profound spiritual energies in the world, and "bringing about a new climate of peace."[19]

The World Council of Churches has as its primary goal of a unified world-wide church. "Eight denominations with over 20,000,000 members recently joined the World Council of Churches."[20]

A Counterfeit Christianity

Vance Havner in his book, *Playing Marbles with Diamonds,* made the following statement: "The devil is not fighting religion. He is too smart for that. He is producing a counterfeit Christianity so much like the real one that good Christians are afraid to speak out against it."[21]

We are plainly told in the Scriptures that in the last days men will not endure sound doctrine and will depart from the truth and heap to themselves teachers to tickle their ears. Jesus said, "And many false prophets shall rise, and shall deceive many" (Matt. 24:11). What will they be like? "There shall be mockers in the last time, who should walk after their own ungodly lusts" (Jude 1:18-19).

Vance Havner has said:

> We are witnessing today the almost complete sell out of the professing church to this pagan world. This is to be expected in the last days of this age as we draw near Babylon; and the Antichrist does not excuse such a sell out, however; what is appalling is that most major churchmen do not seem alarmed. One hears no note of protest, and religious leaders climb on every band

wagon without knowing which way the parade is headed.[22]

Many pastors are afraid that, if they speak according to the Word of God, they will offend someone or turn them off. Some church denominations have gone so far as to rewrite portions of Scripture to keep from offending. Dave Hunts' *CIB Bulletin* reported the following:

> Earlier this year, at its annual convention, the Michigan Episcopal Dioceses refused to vote upon the resolution that "Jesus is the Christ," the only name given under heaven by which we may be saved. The resolution was called "flawed because it presumes to define the ways in which God is able to work," and "divisive and demeaning of people whose faith in God is as strong as ours though it is differently defined." A substitute resolution was voted upon and passed to the effect that Episcopalians would recommit themselves to proclaim a "good news" that offended no one.[23]

In Luke 18:8, Christ asked the question, "Nevertheless, when the Son of man cometh, shall he find faith on the earth?" Will Christ find the real faith or something that has a form of godliness, yet denies God? Will anyone be committed to the real faith, the faith of Jesus Christ?

How will we know who's a true follower of Christ and who is not? Jesus warned us: "Beware of false prophets, who come to you in sheep's clothing, but inwardly they are ravening wolves" (Matt. 7:15). How do you know if someone is a false prophet? They will not speak according to the truth and, "Ye shall know them by their fruits" (7:16).

Lack of discernment allows heresy to enter the Church. Vance Havner said it well when he said, "Nothing is more rare in churches today than discernment."[24] One reason people in the Church are so short on discernment is because they are so lacking in biblical knowledge and personal convictions.

Although heresy and false teaching are evident throughout Christendom, we really should not be surprised. God warns us many times in His Word of the coming deception.

> While evil men and impostors will go from bad to worse, deceiving and being deceived (2 Tim. 3:13).
>
> The Spirit clearly says that in later times some will abandon the faith and follow deceiving spirits and things taught by demons. Such teachings come through hypocritical liars, whose consciences have been seared as with a hot iron (1 Tim. 4:1-2).
>
> For the time will come when men will not put up with sound doctrine. Instead to suit their own desires they will gather around them a great number of teachers to say what their itching ears want to hear (2 Tim. 4:3).

The time of Christ's return is certainly drawing near. All around us, signs of His return can be seen. Jesus said, "Even so, when you see all these things, you know that it is near, right at the door. . . .Therefore keep watch, because you do not know on what day your Lord will come" (Matt. 24:33, 42).

Christ will return, and will be as "a thief in the night" (1 Thess. 5:1-5). For those who have accepted Christ as Lord and Saviour, the thought of His return is glorious. So it is with great anticipation that we say, "Even so, Lord Jesus, quickly come!"

14

A New Commitment: Before It's Too Late!

Let's imagine we have been transported back to 1955. For a few moments try to visualize this post-war period and its culture, people, and values.

Those of us who were not alive then can use images from television re-runs like "Leave It to Beaver," "Father Knows Best," "Dennis the Menace," "I Love Lucy," and "Ozzie and Harriet" to aid our imaginations. That, my friends, despite what the critics say, is how the 1950s really were.

Do you have a feel for the times? Most people don't bother to lock their doors, and kids roam freely up and down the streets without fear of abduction or drive-by shootings.

On school days, elementary children walk to the nearby neighborhood school. After the teacher begins the day by reading a Psalm, the class says the Lord's Prayer out loud and then repeats the Pledge of Allegiance to the flag. On the wall, the Ten Commandments are posted beside a picture of the Good Shepherd holding a tender, young lamb.

At the high school, most students are grade conscious,

and those who have no plans for college study for a trade at the "technical" school or join the armed forces. There are few high school "dropouts", but even they are able to find jobs at the local factories.

Television is a relatively new invention, and most programs revolve around American family life. In fact, an entire family can watch almost any sitcom — or go to the movies together — without fear of being assaulted by filthy curse words, bedroom scenes, or bloody violence.

Teenage pregnancy and babies out of wedlock — even divorce — all are rare occurrences. Hardly anyone has even heard of the word "abortion", and birth control devices are discussed only between a married couple and their doctor.

Sure, the kids may call somebody a "queer", but few have ever met a homosexual. Guys open the doors for their dates, and only "loose" girls call boys on the phone. Most young people get married, have children, and raise a family with the same values they had learned as children.

Back to the Present

Now imagine we jump back into 1993. All the doors are locked and security systems and window bars are a necessity in most cities. Kids never go anywhere alone, and nearly every milk container portrays the sad faces of missing children.

School children rise before the crack of dawn to catch their bus to the racially mixed consolidated facility on the other side of town. At the back of the bus, the older kids smoke and discuss their sexual exploits from the night before.

After passing through a metal detector, the students straggle into their classrooms where the teacher begins the day with a few choice profanities. Prayer is merely a joke since it was banned long before these kids started kindergarten. In fact, the last "nerd" who brought a paperback New Testament to school was suspended for three days and threatened with expulsion if he did it again.

Down the hall at the school "health clinic", a "nurse" begins her day by handing out condoms to a few girls — for some reason the boys never request them. Outside the clinic office, a lonely, depressed teenage girl waits for the dismissal slip that will get her out of classes for the day. She'll be going for her abortion appointment at "Women's Reproductive Services" — arranged by the school nurse and without her parents' permission, of course.

When the bell rings, kids rush out of classrooms and into the hallways, pushing and shoving. The less aggressive students hide in doorways for fear of being punched, grabbed, or even stabbed. No one dares enter the restrooms unless they want to smoke or do drugs.

During the next class, the students gather into groups to finish the "project" they've been working on for weeks. Most are laughing and talking while the teacher tries to maintain some semblance of order. In the back, several students discuss how they will ever get accepted into college since they aren't graded on academic subjects but merely rated on vague "outcomes".

Over at the elementary school, first graders open their reading books to find the ugly face of a scary witch staring back at them from the pages. After a brief discussion on why the witch likes to boil young children in her cauldron, the teacher reads the class a story about a little girl who doesn't have a daddy and whose mommy likes to be affectionate with a woman named Janet.

That evening, the kids watch TV or a rented video in the family room with mom and dad. Amidst a stream of profanity, blasphemy, nudity, and suggestive sexual jokes, they all laugh together without embarrassment. Some stay up to enjoy the late night talk shows, where comedians ridicule every tradition of American society — especially marriage and the church. No one is exempt from their mockery — except liberals and the "politically correct" — and it's open season on every one from conservatives like Dan Qualye to religious leaders like Pope John Paul.

If you were to go from 1955 to 1993 overnight, you would realize how low our culture has sunk in the last 38 years.

You would wonder, *How did we get to this point? Why did we let it happen?*

Let's face it, if the trends continue, our nation will become more and more pagan, depraved, violent, and ignorant. Although the way things are today didn't happen overnight, we still cannot deny the tragic consequences. Like the frog being boiled in the pot, the fire has been turned up so slowly that many of us do not even realize that the American value system is on the verge of extinction. Believe me, we live in desperate times.

We can no longer sit by and watch our nation self-destruct. After reading this book, I hope you have been jolted to take some sort of action. You will either act to help or hurt.

As one person has said, "All it takes for evil to triumph is for good men to do nothing."

No Taboos

Can you imagine the impact Christians would have on their schools, cities, towns, states, and even our country if those who claim to be "born-again" evangelicals would take seriously their Christian commitment?

Christians need to make a new commitment to follow Christ in this new age in which we are living. These are not the days of our parents, grandparents, and especially our great-grandparents. Up until the early sixties most Americans, however, believed in moral absolutes and disapproved of anything that was not consistent with the traditional Protestant faith.

According to an article by the Associated Press, many people today unknowingly hold to New Age beliefs. "While most Americans have never heard of New Age, and most of those who have hold an unfavorable view of it, a surprisingly high proportion accept many of its practices and beliefs."[1] The article provided these statistics:

> • Half of America believe in extrasensory perception, the ability to perceive thoughts or

feelings by other than the five senses.
  • More than a third believe in mental telepa-
thy through which people presumably can communicate their thoughts to others through other
than the five senses.
  • A fourth believe in astrology — that affairs
of their lives may be governed by movement of
planets.
  • About a fifth say they have been in touch to
varying degrees with the dead.

God's Word is very clear that we are to have nothing to
do with such things. In Deuteronomy 18:10-12 we read, "Let
no one be found among you who sacrifices his son or daughter
in the fire, who practices divination or sorcery, interprets
omens, engages in witchcraft, or cast spells, or who is a
medium or spiritualist or who consults the dead."
  We are living in a new age, a new time, when nothing is
taboo. Very few things are considered to be sacred and worthy
of utmost respect and commitment. Not so many years ago,
getting a divorce was considered the breaking of a serious vow
that two people had made before God — a vow to love and to
cherish till death parted them. Today, you can get a divorce at
a drive up window, making the breakup of a marriage as
common and acceptable as ordering a hamburger and fries.
  We live in a society driven by the belief that "I am God
and whatever I believe is morally acceptable." As we have seen
through the previous pages of this book, the two philosophies
of humanism and relativism have, and are having, a profound
effect on our society. The rapid promotion of these philosophies have even desensitized many Christians. Today what
would have horrified our great-grandparents we accept as
commonplace.
  Through the course of history one fact remains the same:
What one generation allows, the next allows a little more.

The Great Rebellion

I truly believe that the New Age is — or plays a big role in — the apostasy of the last days. In 2 Thessalonians 2:3, Paul writes, "For the day will not come until the rebellion occurs and the man of lawlessness is revealed, the man doomed to destruction." The great rebellion must occur before the Antichrist can be revealed. The rebellion is occurring, and people everywhere are being programmed to accept a new leader, a one-world dictator, the Antichrist.

What is an apostasy? The falling away from traditionally held biblical truths and the abandonment of previously held values and beliefs. The New Age movement certainly fits all the characteristics of the apostasy of which the Bible speaks. Why?

> • It has a form of Godliness yet denies God (see 2 Tim. 3:5).
> • It is a movement with a philosophy that promotes the pleasure of men, rather than the love of God (see 2 Tim. 3:4).
> • The New Age movement also promotes the love of self (see 2 Tim. 3:2).
> • The New Age movement shares some of the same goals as the Antichrist, such as: the desire to bring about a one world government, a one world religion, and a one world economical structure.
> • The New Age movement is very active promoting the coming of a world leader.

According to the New Age movement, this world leader will be a modern man concerned about the political, economical, and social problems of our day. He will build a new world. The characteristics and goals of this New Age leader closely match those of the Antichrist as described in Scripture.

God's Word tells us that, during the last days, many impostors will claim to be the Christ and will deceive many before the beast (referring to *the* Antichrist) is revealed. The coming of the lawless one will be in accordance with the work of Satan displayed in all kinds of counterfeit miracles, signs and wonders, and every sort of evil that will deceive those who are perishing.

Why do they perish? Because they refuse to love the truth and be saved. For this reason God sends them a powerful delusion so they will believe the lie. As a result, all will be condemned who have not believed the truth but who have delighted in wickedness.

It is plain to see that Satan's strategy through the New Age movement is to deceive. How does he do this? By tricking them into accepting his humanistic, atheistic, pantheistic, and relativistic lie. Today, Satan is using this deceit to prepare the way for the acceptance of the Antichrist who will be a world leader carrying out the plans and goals of Satan.

Second Thessalonians 2:9-12 states:

> The coming of the lawless one (the Antichrist) will be in accordance with the work of Satan displayed in all kinds of counterfeit miracles, signs, and wonders, and every sort of evil that deceives those who are perishing. They perish because they refused to love the truth and be saved. For this reason God sends them a powerful delusion so that they will believe the lie and so that all will be condemned who have not believed in the truth but have delighted in wickedness.

Before the Antichrist can be revealed, God's Word tells us that a rebellion must occur first. In 2 Thessalonians 2:3 Paul writes, "Don't let anyone deceive you in any way, for that day will not come until the rebellion occurs and the man of lawlessness [the Antichrist] is revealed, the man doomed to destruction." The rebellion that Paul is referring to is the apostasy of the last days. Could we be living in the time of the rebellion?

Standing in the Evil Day

God's Word tells us that we are in a battle that involves "the prince of the power of the air," referring to Satan (Eph. 2:2). We "wrestle not against flesh and blood, but against principalities, against powers, against the rulers of the darkness of this world, against spiritual wickedness in high places" (6:12).

We are not unprotected, however, and God's Word tells us how to stand against the attacks of Satan by putting "on the whole armor of God" (Eph. 6:11). Why? So we will be able to withstand "in the evil day" (6:13). Has there ever been a more evil day than the one in which you and I and our children live?

As this great apostasy takes hold of our land, we need to understand that our renewed commitment to Christ also means a renewed commitment to God's Word. The Word of God has got to be the standard by which we live. Just as you use a ruler to measure inches and feet, we must use the Word of God to measure thoughts and attitudes.

> For the Word of God is living and active. Sharper than any double-edged sword, it penetrates even to dividing soul and spirit, joint and marrow; it judges the thoughts and attitudes of the heart (Heb. 4:12).

We need God's Word to guide us through every day. The Bible is very practical for daily living. "All Scripture is given by inspiration of God, and is profitable for doctrine, for reproof, for correction, for instruction in righteousness" (2 Tim. 3:16).

When we use God's Word as our road map, the trip is so much easier. In fact, Paul tells us in Ephesians 4:14, "Then we will no longer be infants, tossed back and forth by the waves, and blown here and there by every wind of teaching and by the cunning and craftiness of men in their deceitful scheming."

$3 Worth of God?

What was wrong 2,000 years ago according to Scripture is still wrong today. God's Word has not changed over the years to accommodate the devaluing of America. What has changed is our willingness to accept many reprobate activities and lifestyles that are an abomination to God.

The prevailing social attitude is: What is wrong for me may not be wrong for you and vise versa. So, who am I to judge? No wonder our society has declined in "moral quality".

We need a revived dedication to a higher moral standard that is based on God's Word. Vance Havner has said, "Revival begins when we stop justifying ourselves and start judging ourselves."[2]

Christians must come to the realization that the highest calling and greatest reward is found in being the committed disciple Christ talks about in Luke 14:25-35.

In verse 26, Christ says: "If any man will come after Me, and hate not his father, and mother, and wife, and children, and brethren, and sisters, yea, and his own life also, he cannot be My disciple." Christ is simply saying that your love for Him has got to be so great that compared to the love that you have for anyone else, including yourself, it looks like hate.

In verse 27, Christ says, "And whosoever doth not bear his cross and come after Me, cannot be My disciple." The cross of Christ symbolizes the cause of Christ, or in other words, everything that Christ is and stands for.

We must be willing to accept Christ's goals, plans, and desires as ours. Christ makes no bones about this commitment. In fact this is such a serious and radically life changing commitment that in verse 33, Christ tells us that we must be willing to forsake all that we have.

The cause of Christ, especially today, is not popular. Such a radical commitment to Christ and His ways could cost you your reputation, job, or financial well-being — and maybe even your life. This commitment is not to be taken lightly.

Notice that in Luke 14, Christ tells us in three different

verses that if we do not do these things, we are not *good* disciples. Is that what Christ says? No. Jesus says that if you don't do these things, you cannot *be* His disciple.

Five thousand students of the ministry were surveyed recently and asked questions concerning their beliefs on ten major Christian doctrines. Here are the questions and the startling results:

- Do you believe in the physical resurrection?
  Fifty-four percent said no.
- Do you believe in the virgin birth of Christ?
  Fifty-six percent said no.
- Do you believe in the literal heaven and hell?
  Seventy-one percent said no.
- Do you believe in the deity of Jesus Christ?
  Eighty-nine percent said no.
- Do you believe in the depravity of man?
  Ninety-eight percent said no.[3]

What I want to know is why these students are bothering to go into the Christian ministry if they don't believe the teachings of Christ? Do they merely want a "form of religion" while they hold to the precepts of the world?

We need to be completely sold out to God, willing to pay the full price, and not as Wilbur Reese so sarcastically writes,

> I would like $3 worth of God please. Not enough to explode my soul or disturb my sleep, but just enough to equal a cup of warm water, or a snooze in the sunshine. I don't want enough of Him to make me love a black man, or pick beets with a migrant. I want ecstasy not transformation, I want the warmth of the womb, not a new birth. I want about a pound of the eternal in a paper sack. I would like to buy $3 worth of God please. [4]

Our new commitment for this new age needs to be a commitment to follow Christ no matter the cost.

No Retreats, No Reserves, No . . .

Bill Borden's father founded Borden Industries, which at one time was the nation's largest dairy producer. Upon graduating from high school, Bill's parents gave him a cruise around the world.

Not long after he began his travels, the Bordens received a letter in which Bill described how his heart filled with compassion for the people whom he met. No matter what country they were from, no matter what color they were, or what language they spoke, Bill saw they had one thing in common: they needed Jesus Christ.

Bill's second letter came to his parents with the request to pray for him because he felt that the Lord might be calling him into full-time mission work. Finally, Bill's third letter brought the news that he had committed his life to preaching the gospel to the lost and dying.

After Bill returned home, he enrolled at Yale, and four years later graduated among the top in his class. Not long after Bill's graduation, his father became ill and was no longer able to run Borden Industries.

In need of a qualified leader, the chairman of the board came to Bill and asked if he would take his father's place. After all, Bill was a Borden, was familiar with the business, and had graduated among the top of his class. He was the obvious choice. Although flattered by the offer, Bill requested some time to pray and think about his answer.

A few days later, Bill explained to the board that he greatly appreciated the offer, but he had made the commitment to go into full-time missions work, and thus felt that he should fulfill his commitment. Bill turned down everything the world holds dear: power, position, prestige, money. Bill gave that all up because of his commitment.

It is said that Bill took his Bible and turned to the back page where he wrote the two words, NO RETREATS. That reminds me of the hymn, "I have decided to follow Jesus, no turning back, no turning back, though no one join me, still I will follow, no turning back, no turning back."

Bill enrolled in seminary, and, feeling the need to live by faith, raised his own support. In fact, any money he received from his wealthy family in the way of allowance, he gave away. Then, Bill took his Bible and below the two words, NO RETREATS, he wrote, NO RESERVES. Holding nothing back, he trusted the Lord wholeheartedly.

Upon graduating from seminary, Bill boarded a ship that took him to Egypt where he planned to study a group of people much like those he would be working with in the future. While in Egypt, Bill contracted meningitis, and before his family could reach him, he died.

Many people said, "What a waste. Bill could have had it all, but he gave it all up to go to a foreign land where he contracted a disease and died without any family." But it was not a waste. Bill Borden did not die in vain.

The story of Bill Borden rang around the world, and thousands of young people picked up the call and replaced Bill on the mission field. Because of one committed life, others went into full-time mission work and thus, thousands of people came to know Christ as their personal Lord and Saviour. All it took was one committed life, and thousands were changed for eternity.

When Bill's family finally received his personal effects, among them they found his Bible. Upon turning to the last page they saw the two words, NO RETREATS. Below those two words they read, NO RESERVES. And as though scrawled on his death bed they found the two new words, NO REGRETS.

Even though Bill has not walked the face of this earth for nearly 75 years, the story of Bill's life and commitment is still challenging lives for Jesus Christ today.

A Splinter in the Forest

If we serve Christ wholeheartedly, in the end we will have no regrets. This life is tough, and it has many discouraging moments; but in the end — if we remain faithful and committed to Christ and His cause — it will have been worth it all.

As the apostle Paul wrote, "For I consider that the sufferings of this present time is not worthy to compare to the glory that shall be revealed in us" (Rom. 8:18-21). Did you catch that? This life is so short, that compared to the length and rewards of eternity, this life and all its hardships are not even worthy of comparison to the glory that will be revealed in us.

Upon completing a seminar in Great Falls, Montana, a gentleman walked up to me and slipped a small piece of paper into my hand, smiled, and walked away. Since it was not uncommon for people to slip me little notes, I simply tucked it away to read later. Back at my hotel, as I began to empty my suit coat pockets, I came across this little folded piece of paper.

I carefully opened this note to read nine words I'll not soon forget. "Life is a splinter in the forest of eternity."

That's it folks, this life will soon be over, and eternity will then begin. We have such a short time to accomplish that which will last forever. This causes me to ask myself, "What am I doing today that will effect eternity?"

Jim Elliot, one of the missionaries killed by the Indians in Equador, said it best: "He is no fool who gives what he cannot keep to gain that which he cannot lose." Or, as the old hymn says, "One life will soon be past, only what's done for Christ will last."

Let us continue to run the race and fight the good fight. Take your place on the battlefield to which God has called you.

Our fight, however, is not against the humanistic educational establishment, the New Age movement, or the coming of a one-world government. These things have been prophesied to happen. They must come to pass because Scripture *will* be fulfilled.

What then is our goal? Our mission is the same as it has always been: to be committed disciples who are striving to fulfill the Great Commission.

Parents, we must take those young lives God has given us and mold them into disciples for Him and His service. During those crucial years from cradle to college, let us instill into our children the truths of Jesus Christ.

We all need the kind of commitment that Hanna Whitall Smith called, "reckless abandonment for Christ." When we have lived such a life for Christ, we can then look with pride at the generation coming after us and say, "No regrets!"

Note from the author . . .

I want to make it perfectly clear that I am all for, and on the side of, conservative teachers. We need more conservative teachers teaching within our public educational system.

I do not want this book to discourage you, but to strengthen your resolve for staying in the battle. Parents need you, and most importantly, our children need you.

Keep up the good work!

Ambassadors for the Family

Interviews with William Bennett, Gary Bauer, Jack Kemp, Congressman Robert Dornan, and Phyllis Schlafly

The people interviewed here are on the frontlines fighting for the traditional family and traditional values. This chapter is from exclusive interviews that I personally conducted with these distinguished family advocates. I think you will find what they have to say to be insightful, thought provoking, encouraging, and filled with wisdom gained through experience and first hand observation.

William Bennett

William Bennett served as secretary of theDepartment of Education as well as chairman of the National Endowment for the Humanities under the Reagan Administration. Under President Bush, Mr. Bennett also served as the director of the Office of National Drug Control Policy.

Today, as co-director of Empower American, Mr. Bennett serves along with former congressman and HUD secretary in the Bush Administration, Jack Kemp. As if that were not enough Mr. Bennett is currently a John M. Olin Fellow at the Hudson Institute as well as a Distinguished Fellow in Cultural Policy Studies at the Heritage Foundation. On top of all that, he is a senior editor for the popular conservative magazine, *National Review.*

Brannon: *Many Americans were happy to hear about the formation of Empower America, headed by you and Jack Kemp. What are some of the goals of this organization and how can other conservatives aid you in this cause?*

Bennett: We hope to give people the opportunity to join Empower America over the next few months. The purpose of the organization is to advance conservative principles in three major areas.

The first is foreign policy. We seek an active involvement of the United States in the world. We don't think it's time for America to retreat from responsibilities of leadership.

Second, we believe in the entrepreneurial spirit of democratic capitalism, smaller government, lower taxes, and taking the steps to grow this economy.

Third, we believe in cultural renewal. We have to address social and cultural issues, particularly as they center on the family to improve this part of American life.

Brannon: *The traditional Judeo Christian family is being severely attacked today by the education establishment and Hollywood. The attempt is to try and prove that the traditional family just does not exist. This is contrary to the fact that the Census Bureau reports that 70 percent of children today are being raised in a two-parent home. Why is this such an important message for the liberal left to try to convey?*

Bennett: Because they want to challenge the idea of the traditional family to give people excuses for not meeting their own responsibilities. I would agree with your number, but I would also agree that the family is in some trouble because of the assault by the media, by Hollywood, and by others. The rates of divorce and family dissolution are not encouraging.

Brannon: *What do you think are some of the goals that the secular humanists want to accomplish today through the American educational system?*

Bennett: They want to rid the world, essentially, of the

Judeo Christian tradition and its influences. And they are doing this by trying to get all references to this tradition, as it is taught, out of American classrooms. But the American story without the Judeo Christian tradition is a much paltrier story. Indeed, you cannot tell the story without that tradition.

Brannon: *You can talk about Buddha and have a book about Buddha in the classroom, but you can't have the Bible, which holds the standards upon which our country was founded.*

Bennett: That is correct. Indeed, it is the most important book in Western civilization, whether one is a believer or not. It is a fact that the Bible is the most consequential book in Western civilization and it is the one book that cannot be read in America's classrooms.

Brannon: *In an article by* Time *magazine the statement was made that educators want to develop a curriculum to foster respect for all religions and lifestyles. But I think that is a contradictory statement because they are not trying to foster respect and acceptance for the lifestyle of the traditional Judeo Christian. Would you agree with that?*

Bennett: The last form of acceptable bigotry in our society is bigotry toward the evangelical Christian who seeks to make his religion part of the world. This is a form of bigotry that I have seen a lot of, particularly among the liberal elite and it's quite horrible to see.

Brannon: *You also said in your book,* The Devaluing of America, *"The truth of the real world is that without standards and judgments, there can be no progress." If I didn't know better, I would think that you were referring to Outcome Based Education and its 51 politically correct goals and achievements. What is your assessment of this value-based program?*

Bennett: I am in favor of Outcome Based Education if we are measuring real outcomes that are truly measurable and are of importance to parents, like the children's ability to read, write, count, and think. But that is not, as you know, what people measure in Outcome Based Education.

I would like to see national standards where we are able to test and assess students on their ability to compute, do science, read, and write. But that would be a serious set of standards not the strange and irrelevant ones that are proposed in the OBE theory.

Brannon: *That leads me to my next question. You mention in your book that we need reliable national standards for education and students must be tested by those standards. Currently, all the national assessment tests are voluntary. Do you feel that such national testing should be made mandatory, and if so, why, and if not, why?*

Bennett: Well, it's tricky and it's risky because one worries about control of these tests. Nevertheless, I think it would be worthwhile to explore the possibilities, provided you could keep these tests free of ideology, political bias, and political correctness. I would like to take the temperature of American children, for example, in things like knowledge of mathematics. But, I would probably stay away from English and history because the chances of them being corrupted are too great.

Brannon: *Give me your assessment of America 2000. Do you feel that it is as potentially dangerous as do many of its critics?*

Bennett: Yes, to the degree that it will lead us to a homogenized and low level of education. America 2000 has a set of goals that are thoroughly unrealistic, and this isn't the way to solve American education. The way to solve America's education problems is real accountability, real standards, and educational choice for all parents.

Brannon: *From what we understand, the program has not changed, the name is the same, and everything is going forward. The only change is that they have taken out parental choice. Why are the liberals so opposed to school choice and the voucher system?*

Bennett: Because it will break up the power structure of the liberal establishment, which rests in the teachers unions and the education establishment.

Brannon: *Do you feel that the educational system and its elite — along with the NEA — are out of touch with American* *parents and their concerns and desires?*

Bennett: There is no question that the leadership is out of touch with American parents. The only way to get them back in touch is to let the parents make the decisions: a) about where their children go to school, b) what their children are taught, and c) what their children are tested on.

Brannon: *In your book you said that the education establishment opposes reform because it is interested in maintaining power. What do you think they hope to do with this power?*

Bennett: They want to enhance their own self interests. They want to raise teachers salaries. They want to influence their clout at the federal trough and at the State trough, but the interests of children are way down on their list of priorities.

Brannon: *In 1978 you wrote an excellent article with Edwin Delattire titled, "Moral Education in the Schools," regarding values clarification courses. Very briefly, what do you feel are some of the dangers of values clarification courses and why are these courses more popular today than when you wrote the article?*

Bennett: Values clarification, I think, was the single worst idea in American education in the late sixties and early seventies. It said there is no such thing as right or wrong. Unfortunately, many children learned that in American schools and have acted on it. It has proved to be a catastrophic teaching. It is still taught very widely in American schools because it is easy and people can argue that they are responding to the need for "values education." But of course, this is not values education. This is a travesty. This is not an education in morality. It is simply an education in wants and desires. It is the opposite of moral education.

Brannon: *For my final question, what can the concerned conservative parent do to make for a better and more traditional educational system?*

Bennett: Pull their children out of their schools if they don't like them and try to get them into other schools. Teach them at home if that is their preference. Work hard to achieve educational choice and raise cane with the local authorities. We will get there. Persevere. This is America. We can change it.

Brannon: *I want to thank you Mr. Bennett. I really respect what you are doing, and I'm looking forward to your next book. I think you are doing a fine job, and I really appreciate it.*

William Bennett with Brannon Howse.

Gary Bauer

Gary Bauer served as the under secretary of education under William Bennett and as an assistant to President Reagan for Policy Development and director of the Office of Policy Development in the White House until he resigned in October, 1988.

Bauer is now the president of the Family Research Council, and a senior vice president with Focus on the Family. The Family Research Council is a conservative lobbying group for the traditional family in Washington, DC.

Brannon: *Please give us the traditional definition of the traditional family and the government's definition of the traditional family.*

Bauer: The interesting point is that it is very common now in newspaper articles or in school board meetings to have somebody stand up and say, "Well this is not the fifties anymore. We are not dealing with Ozzie and Harriet. In fact only 6 to 10 percent of American families fit the traditional definition." Most people hear that and think, "Good grief, I didn't realize that American families have changed that much."

About a year ago, we started looking into how they came up with that number, whether it is 6 percent or 10 percent. We discovered that liberals are so narrowly defining what the traditional family is, that they are leaving out millions of households that would normally consider themselves traditional. The definition they use to get this low number includes a husband who works, a wife who stays home all day, and their two children. That is how they get the 6 percent figure or 10 percent figure, depending on which calculation they use.

If you have three children, you are not a traditional family. If you have one child, you are not a traditional family. If your children are grown up and have gone on to college, you are not traditional. If your wife works even one hour outside the home in either volunteer or paid work, you are not traditional.

They have come up with an obviously ludicrous yardstick to define "traditional." Then they constantly repeat the figure over and over again, that somewhere between 6 to 10 percent of American families are traditional. The result is that if I go to a Congressional hearing to testify and argue for traditional values, I will have well-meaning congressmen say, "Well, Mr. Bauer, I agree with you, but as you know, only 10 percent of our families are traditional." They have read the same material that has been repeated over and over again, and they have assumed that it is accurate.

In fact, the great majority of the American people live in households headed by a married couple. The great majority of American people are, by most any definition, traditional.

It is true that about 25 percent of the children born this year will be born out of wedlock, and that is a terrible development. But even if you go to those households, you will often find a young woman who hopes for her child very traditional things. You will find a young woman often hoping she will find a man who will fulfill a commitment to her, marry her, and help her have the kind of household that people have always wanted. You'll see in most cases, those young women hoping for their children the same values that we hope for our kids.

The major point to be made here is that there is a concerted effort under way to redefine traditional in such a way that those of us who do live in traditional families will feel like we are a small remnant that is about ready to disappear. That, however, is just not the case.

Brannon: *What is the purpose of the Family Research Council?*

Bauer: We are in the middle trying to do two things. On one end, we have are our grassroots constituents outside of Washington, DC, and they need information about what is going on in the nation's capital. Through publications like *Washington Watch,* and special bulletins, we try to tell these grassroots individuals about issues that may affect them, their schools, and neighborhoods. We tell them where they can write or phone to have some influence on public policy.

On the other hand, we have an establishment here in Washington that often doesn't know the concerns of average families. Therefore, I go and testify before congressional committees. We have full-time lobbyists who walk the halls of Congress in order to lobby congressmen for various issues that we are concerned about. We routinely go to the White House and meet with people there in an attempt to get them to move their policies in a certain direction. And probably the other third of our time, we spend with the media.

In an average week, I do about 25 or 30 interviews with newspaper journalist, and radio and TV reporters, trying to promote the pro-family agenda and get it out there in a favorable way so that Americans, who haven't really focused on it yet, will have a good idea what we are about and what we are trying to accomplish.

Brannon: *As former assistant aecretary of education under the Reagan Administration, what is your assessment of America 2000?*

Bauer: I think the plan is well-intentioned. There are some good ideas in it as far as goals and where we are going to reach academic performance. But it fails to make a number of key reforms that have to be made concerning choice and accountability — whether accountability of teachers or more testing in the classroom.

It has a number of elements in it that are too centralized for my taste. I think the worst thing that we could do is centralize the running of American Education here in Washington, DC. We can look at every other area that Washington has touched, whether it is housing or whatever, and they have made a shambles out of it. The last thing we want to do is put in the power of federal bureaucrats the right to make decisions about what goes on in our local school districts.

Brannon: *What is your response to those who say that the conservative camp should not scream about America 2000 because it is really about less government control?*

Bauer: Initially, some parts of the program would have resulted in less government control, but, unfortunately, they immediately caved in on those things when they sent the legislation to capitol hill. There was a choice provision in the America 2000 legislation. Ted Kennedy, however, made it clear that he wouldn't let that choice provision get out of his committee unless the administration dropped it and went on to try and cut a deal. If they were serious in the effort to decentralize, they should have made it clear to Kennedy that there would be no education bill unless the provisions for educational choice remained in the bill. Failing to do that, sent the signal to us that they are not that serious about issues like choice.

Brannon: *What are some of the key potential dangers of America 2000?*

Bauer: It is hard to put down all the specific things that can go wrong. The bottom line is that for about 35-40 years now, we have had larger and larger educational bureaucracy. We have had more and more money spent on education, and we have had poorer and poorer results with our kids, both in areas like reading and writing — which are basic educational goals — and the kind of value systems children leave school with.

We don't see anything in America 2000 that is likely to interrupt those trends. In fact, in some of the ideas in the program, we think the trends toward more bureaucracy and more money and very little outcome could even be accelerated. America 2000 doesn't make the kind of radical changes that the core of American education needs in order to get out of the mess we are in right now.

Brannon: *What do you feel those changes should be?*

Bauer: I think the most important one is the school choice idea because we effectively have a monopoly as far as most parents are concerned. There are education alternatives out there, but they are often so costly that most parents have only one provider to choose from and that is the local public school. As long as that is the situation, we are going to have a bad outcome, just as if we gave General Motors the only right to manufacture and sell a car in the United States. We would have a pretty lousy car after a number of years.

If the educational system is opened up, we will end up ultimately with a better public school system. In fact, the best way to be pro-public education is to push for competition because ultimately it will be the best thing for public education.

Beyond that, there is all sorts of research about what works in schools, and yet, educators tend to ignore the research. For example, we know that if teachers regularly assign kids homework and — if they actually do the homework and don't subcontract it out to their parents — those kids get better grades. Yet a lot of American classrooms and schools are still locked into the idea that homework is oppressive and that it is unfair to monopolize the kids' time outside the classroom.

Another example is competency testing for teachers. As long as we don't have a system in place that can regularly measure a teacher's knowledge and his or her ability to transmit that knowledge in the classroom, we are going to continue to have teachers who are not capable of teaching our kids.

Merit pay is also a good idea. There ought to be a system in place where good teachers who perform are paid more than mediocre teachers. This has only been experimented with in about twenty school districts around the country, and some of those are beginning to cut it back.

Finally, there is the whole issue of values. There is a consensus among the American people that schools ought to be reinforcing reliable standards of right and wrong, yet the educational establishment is in the throws of the notion that not only is that something they should not be doing, but they don't believe there are such standards. As long as we have that kind of foolishness, where teachers, counselors, and others are sending the message that there are no reliable standards of right and wrong, we are going to get the results that we are seeing in kids today.

Brannon: *Phyllis Schlafly said she believes that this national curriculum is less about academic achievement and more about attitudes, emotions, and values. Do you agree?*

Bauer: Yes, if you look at the trend in recent years in the educational establishment and the educational bureaucracy. There is a tendency for them to get into those areas. If there was a national curriculum, I'm afraid that would happen.

Secretary Alexander Meadows, has talked about the need to come up with standard courses. There are rational arguments to be made for that. In a perfect world, it might be a good thing to do. It is disturbing when kids in Appalachia are getting a lower standard of educational material than kids in Fairfax county Virginia. In a perfect world, everyone would like to even out those differences. But as long as we have a centralized educational system, the danger is that somebody's values or somebody's hidden agenda is going to drive that curriculum and tilt that curriculum. Until we come up with something like educational choice, we cannot afford to let educators federalize or nationalize things like school curriculum.

Brannon: *What would you want Christian Americans to place at the top of their prayer list regarding the family and the traditional family values?*

Bauer: I would put on the top to pray for forgiveness for our country. If you look at the vision our founding fathers had of virtuous people who would be capable of self-government, a lot has happened since that early idea and a lot has gone very wrong. Just as Lincoln used to look at slavery and pray that God would be merciful with America because of that plight, I would hope that we would pray that God would be merciful with us about other things, like abortion, that we are perpetuating. Beyond that, I can't think of something better to pray for than a national revival.

Lincoln said that in a democracy, public opinion is everything. He was right. If we are unhappy about the way things have gone in recent years, part of it has to be attributed to the fact that this is what people have voted. Until they start voting differently and can sort out their own values, nothing will change. Unless people realize what our forefathers were trying to create and preserve those ideas for the future, we are going to continue to have the kinds of messes that we have seen in the last couple of years with members of Congress bouncing checks, etc.

I could get into all kinds of other specific issues that people ought to be praying about such as the abortion issue, etc. But I think the two areas of mercy for our country and revival for our people would be the two things I would put at the top.

Brannon: *I noticed last year you were on "Nightline" with two men who were redefining the family up in New York. As the pro-homosexual agenda continues to manifest itself in the media and through television shows, the battle seems to be very difficult in the media. What kind of headway do you perceive as far as states maintaining holds on sodomy laws? Do you see an erosion there to a great extent?*

Bauer: In almost every area of public policy that we deal with, I am relatively optimistic. With the abortion issue, we are making progress. The other side gets up every day having lost a little bit more and is worried about what the court is going to do. I could go down the list in almost every area and see positive trends taking place — except for the radical gay rights agenda. On that, I think we are thoroughly on the defensive.

They are well on their way to redefining homosexuality as being an alternative lifestyle and homosexuals as being a protected minority. It is particularly pronounced on university campuses. Even in some of the most otherwise conservative schools in the country, students are being taught that to oppose homosexuality in the nineties is the equivalent of being in the Klu Klux Klan in the fifties.

We get a constant stream of letters from students, some of whom have been interns here, from places like Vanderbuilt, Duke, and the University of Pennsylvania, which are schools which you would not associate with a radical agenda. The letters are always the same. The gay rights people on these campuses are powerful, and the school administrations are very sympathetic to them. Students who speak out against the homosexual agenda are in danger of being kicked out of school under political correctness. We have a major battle there, and the nineties will determine how that battle comes out.

Brannon: *In your book,* Children at Risk, *you said that Hollywood is the weapon in our cultural civil war. Its values*

Hollywood is the weapon in our cultural civil war. Its values in the guise of entertainment are promoted in our living rooms and on thousands of movie screens. Our children are particularly influenced by the value messages they receive that ridicule traditional beliefs and undercut commitment to family and faith. How can Judeo-Christians protect traditional values in today's society?

Bauer: That is a good question. There are all kinds of things that we can and should do. It's important to spend time with like-minded people. It's important for us to hold each other up and socialize with people who have the same values that we do. There is safety in numbers. Because a lot of people feel that they are surrounded by hostile territory, it's necessary to develop a common cause and help them understand that many millions of Americans believe in family and Christian values.

I think it's important for parents to have the courage to be parents. That means saying no, and having your teenager being upset. I have a teenager, and she knows how to stomp up the steps and slam the door, which is what teenagers are supposed to know how to do, but parents are supposed to know how to say no. A lot of parents sometimes just can't find the courage to swim against the tide when faced with the argument that everybody is doing this or everybody is going here. A lot of parents cave in rather than risk having their child singled out as being different. So we have to get our own values straight before we can expect our kids to do the right things.

Obviously, living a life with faith and working on that aspect is very important. Spending time with your kids is key. Parents, all kinds of parents, are guilty of this. Good Christian parents are guilty of having high-power jobs and not being there at dinner time and not having time to talk with their kids about problems, etc.

When I was working at the White House, I had an agreement with my wife that I would come home for dinner just to make sure that we had that time together as a family — even if that meant driving back into work after dinner. We really wise. We can't assume that an hour a week of quality time is going to make up for all the other influences.

Brannon: *What is your view of the correct role of the Department of Education and the power it should have?*

Bauer: I think the Department of Education can be an agency for researching what is working around the country. If something is working well in a school district in Alabama, then I could see the Department of Education playing a role in taking that example and sharing it with other school districts. If something is not working some place else, they ought to share the information of what doesn't work so that every school district doesn't have to make the same mistakes.

When I was working in the Department of Education, we had a study done by businessmen on how to efficiently run the department. We found was that we could run the entire Department of Education with about 900 employees. At the time, we had 10,000. Over two years we got it down to 8,000. Now it is up to 12,000-14,000. What we don't need in that department is a large and growing bureaucracy that thinks it knows how to run local schools better than the people who live in those communities.

Brannon: *What were some of your goals and projects that you held dear and worth fighting for as under secretary of education?*

Bauer: We did a lot of speaking about the need to teach reliable standards of right and wrong and get values clarification out of the classroom. I did a study of American textbooks and how they handled various issues and then went to the national convention of textbook publishers. Instead of giving them the normal speech they expected from an education official, which is one of these sort of pat-on-the-back speeches, I announced the results of my study and charged them with failing American education. It caused an incredible controversy and all kinds of congressional committees. They haven't invited me back since.

Brannon: *As senior vice president of Focus on the Family and president of Family Resource Council, what words*

*of encouragement would you give to the traditional family who
sees all the relativism in morality, humanism, atheism, etc.?*

Bauer: Families need to remember that the way we have
chosen to live is not only ordained by God, but it works. What
we see around us is a failure of these alternative systems. As
they continue to fail, I think we can count, a little bit at least,
on common sense winning out. As young people see more of
their friends dying from things like AIDS, that may do more to
reinstill sexual morality than anything we are likely to do in this
debate we are in right now.

I would also remind people that this is not a hundred-yard
dash. It is a marathon. Things are not going to get better in a
day, or a week, or a month, or a year. We didn't get into this fix
overnight, and we are not going to get out of it overnight. I
would encourage people to keep the faith to be Christian
citizens and talk to their neighbors and friends about what we
believe and assume that, ultimately, the common sense of our
fellow citizens will win out.

Jack Kemp

Brannon: *With the increased invasion of the federal government into the lives of the American citizens, what can concerned individuals do to stop this unwanted intrusion?*

Kemp: The most important is to speak up, and the second is to elect men and women to the Congress and to the state legislative houses and senates who understand that there is no substitute for the family. The government cannot be the mother, the father, the parent, and try to do everything for everybody. It can't be a nanny because it sublimates the basic role of the family.

Thirdly, we should introduce the idea of subjecting all legislation to several criteria, one of which should be: How does it impact on the traditional family? What does it do?

Does our welfare system support the family? Does it cause it to be disruptive? I make a case that the welfare system is anti-family because it rewards families who break up and punishes families who come together. It punishes people who have children and needs to be radically overhauled to make it family supportive not family destructive.

Brannon: *What are a few missing components that would help to create a more competitive and quality educational system?*

Kemp: More choice! Give parents, as Polly Williams is doing in downtown Milwaukee, a chance to get access to private as well as public schools. I think Magnet schools are very important in providing educational choice in the public school system. I was a champion of that in Buffalo when I was in the Congress.

When the parents are involved in choosing where they send their precious children, they take a greater interest. When principals are more accountable to parents and more accountable for the quality of the education that the students receive, they will be more likely to hire good teachers. With choice, I believe we will have a much better educational system in America.

We need more competition for the public school, and it can only come from private schools, whether they are Jewish, Catholic, evangelical, private, or secular.

Brannon: *In a speech in April in Washington, DC, you closed your address by saying, "I read the end and we win." This is a quote that I have heard before, and I have used over the last couple of years in my seminar entitled "The Traditional Family's Quest for Survival." What do you mean by this statement?*

Kemp: I am a Christian. My family are Christians. We do not think that there is any room in Judeo Christian theology or philosophy for pessimism. We have problems, but they should be met boldly and audaciously.

I have read both Hebrew and Christian Scripture and when I say that I have read the last chapter, I was alluding to the fact that the history of the Bible is the history of a few people overcoming great armies, great nations, and great powers. I believe that we can overcome these obstacles. I am an optimist. Besides, you can't play quarterback in the NFL and be a pessimist.

Brannon: *Since the majority of our readers in this book will be concerned conservatives, what would your personal message be to them?*

Kemp: That their conservatism has to be both vertical and horizontal. It has to be vertical in terms of its values. They need to know where those values come from. There is no such thing as relativism when it comes to the truth, ethics, morality, or honesty, and those eternal values.

On the other hand conservatism has to be progressive in terms of working for change, reform, and a better future, not only for this country but for the whole world. Not only for the whole world but for our inner cities and to bring more people into an opportunity to be conservative.

A lot of people don't like conservatism because they don't have anything to conserve. They have yet to get a stack in the system. They don't own any property; they don't have a job; they don't have a home; they don't have a chance to send their children to a good school. You can't expect people who don't own anything to be as defensive of the system that you and I take for granted.

I am a great believer that conservatives should be part of a movement and a reform effort to spread ownership and entrepreneurship and opportunity and education and pro-family values. That's what we must do if we expect to win more people to our cause.

Brannon Howse interviewing Jack Kemp.

Congressman Robert Dornan

Brannon: *As the father of five, and the grandfather of nine, what things most concern you about the future of your children and grandchildren living here in America and attending the educational system that we have today?*

Dornan: My number one worry is what President Reagan addressed on January 11, nine days before he left office and George Bush was sworn in. He said he dreaded the failure of American society to teach succeeding generations all of the great history of our country, the good and the bad, and the adventure of making the world's most incredible nation in all of recorded history. That's what I see — the not passing on of the great history and traditions of the United States of America.

The other is not teaching young people anything about the world around them — what makes cultures and civilizations different, the roots and basis of western civilization, Greek history, Roman history, the whole story of Christendom, and western civilization based on Christianity, the history of the Jewish people from the Old Testament right down to modern times. Most young people aren't learning about all the things that have made this civilization such an exciting adventure.

Brannon: *In Colorado a teacher was not even allowed to have the Bible in his private library on his desk. The Supreme Court, however, refused to hear the case that would have at least made it possible to use the Bible as a piece of literature. Bill Bennett has said that the Bible is still the most important book in our western culture. What do you think?*

Dornan: Abraham Lincoln said the two things he studied most in his youth to give him a command of the English language were the Bible and Shakespeare. Whether it was Edward Devere, the seventeenth Earl of Oxford, or this poor man of humble origin, William Shakespeare — whichever one wrote all of those magnificent 39 plays — quotes from the

Bible are all through his works. To not teach the Bible as a masterful work of literature is to deprive young Americans of a full education.

Brannon: *What does the appointment of Jocelyn Elders as surgeon general say about the Clinton Administration?*

Dornan: I think his social appointments tell far more about the man than the careful way he's approached national appointments. President Clinton knows that if he is going remake this country into the image he dreamed about in his early post-college years in Arkansas and make all his visions come to pass, his social appointments in the areas of education, welfare, health, and human services are critical. He knows that if he were to make similar radical appointments in defense, national security, and legal areas that he would become a one-term president.

His social appointments give the full picture Clinton's radical agenda. What has absolutely appalled me is the lack of courage of half of the Republicans in the Senate. There are no alarm bells going off among the Republicans in the Senate as to how radically Clinton is shifting this country to the left across the whole social spectrum.

Brannon: *We touched on President Clinton's education as a young man. Are you familiar with his governor's school in Arkansas?*

Dornan: Yes. That was brought to me during the campaign. We went over all that and had the articles, but we couldn't get anybody in the Bush campaign interested. That should have been a national issue during the presidential race.

Brannon: *Do you have a few thoughts that you would like to leave with my readers concerning the battles the traditional family is fighting when it comes to education, as well as the ongoing fight for mere survival?*

Dornan: We have not passed the point of no return. I meet people all the time who say that we have. That there is no rebuilding, that we have gone too far, that the American dream has been destroyed by the liberal and radical philosophy.

In the beginning of 1992 we had 253.6 million people in

America. Even if only half the population believed in traditional family values, we could accomplish anything as a country. But nobody can make a case to me that half this country is opposed to the values that I was raised with. You just can't. If it were 10 percent, I would be amazed. But that 10 percent is mostly affected by the mass media. And that's what gives the impression that all is lost.

Even if fifty or sixty million people in America have no religious foundation and no belief or knowledge in Western civilization, then it would still be only a quarter of the population. Why should three-fourths of the nation surrender to a quarter? And I believe it's more like 85 or 90 percent against 10 or 15 percent. Why should we surrender?

I'm in this fight, knock-down, drag-out, right to the end. Since I truly believe that numbers are in our favor and that there is a sleeping giant out there that we've just got to wake up. If we don't pass this on, our message, to the next generation, we're going to be pretty miserable when we are sitting in our rocking chairs on a porch somewhere.

Phyllis Schlafly

Brannon: *Why did you begin Eagle Forum and what is its purpose?*

Mrs. Schlafly: In 1972, I formed a committee to stop passage of the Equal Rights Amendment. That developed into an extremely successful campaign that extended over ten years. After ERA was defeated, we realized that there were many other issues that our members were interested in. That is why we formed Eagle Forum, and now we work on a whole range of conservative and pro-family issues.

Brannon: *How can conservatives be more influential in getting people to think through the consequences of socialism as we see it rising today?*

Mrs. Schlafly: Conservatives should engage in political action. Our founding fathers gave us a wonderful system of self-government, and if conservatives and pro-family types do not participate in the process, you can be sure that other people will who do not share our values. I urge all conservatives to be active in the political process, in the election of candidates, in lobbying for legislation, and in expressing our views on the media.

Brannon: *Among such curriculum such as* Quest, *and* Do So, *and the* Impressions *program, which is being used most widely across the country?*

Mrs. Schlafly: I don't have any figures on how many schools use them, but all of them are extremely widely used in all parts of the country. They are all psychological curriculum that many of us find extremely offensive. We send children to school to learn how to read and write, add and subtract, spell, and acquire some knowledge of our country, our government, and science. There is no place for group therapy in the public school classroom, or for psychological courses that are not academic.

Brannon: *Aren't these programs values clarification courses?*

Mrs. Schlafly: They are a version of values clarification, that is correct. Value clarification is very much a misnomer. All it really does is clarify their wants and desires. It doesn't clarify any values at all. The whole purpose of values clarification, as it is taught, is to teach the child that there is no eternal truth nor stable and enduring values and that whatever the child decides and is comfortable with is okay. That is very a bad thing to teach children.

It is called "undirective education," and it means that the adults have defaulted on the job and decided that they are not going to give their children the wisdom and benefit of adult experience.

Brannon: *Values clarification is being promoted by the liberal elite within the context of Outcome Based Education. Can you give me a quick analysis of OBE?*

Mrs. Schlafly: OBE is an attempt to replace academic training with discussion of emotion and attitudes and behavior. There is no accountability in it. The parents have no idea of what the child is learning or what he has accomplished. It is an attempt to deceive the parents about what is going on in the public school classroom. Again, we believe that psychological course and behavior modification have no place in the public school classroom.

Brannon: *OBE will be implemented nationally by goal #3 of the six national goals listed in the program of America 2000. Knowing that you have written editorials for the* Washington Post *and other publications on the subject of America 2000, could you share with me some of the most dangerous aspects?*

Mrs. Schlafly: Most people don't have any idea what America 2000 means. It can really mean whatever the people implementing it choose it to mean. It can be implemented through OBE, or it can be implemented through all sorts of other trendy educational fads that come along.

I don't believe America 2000 and OBE are synonymous. America 2000 is a cover word used to lend some respectability to any kind of change that the schools feel like adopting.

OBE has a very clear pattern of replacing academic work with attitudinal objective. OBE wants to replace the traditional Carnegie unit of measuring success in a high school with an nebulous arrangement in which the parents will never know what their children were taught.

Brannon: *Can you explain, from the research of Eagle Forum, why you consider Parents as Teachers to be a dangerous program?*

Mrs. Schlafly: The America 2000 booklet is vague as to which programs will be implemented. I think the first goal of America 2000, which is that every child will start school ready to learn, is extremely ominous. How is the government going to deal with children before they go to school? I don't think that it is any of the government's business what happens to the child before he goes to school. I think the job of the government through the public school system is to teach children to read after they are an appropriate age and in school.

We find the Parents as Teachers Program extremely objectionable. Parents as Teachers should be called Teachers as Parents. Schools are trying to substitute as parents and take over the raising of the children from infancy, something that the government and the schools have no competence to do. It should not be part of America 2000, even under the best of circumstances.

Brannon: *In your opinion what is the greatest threat to home schoolers today?*

Mrs. Schlafly: The greatest threat comes from the national education system, which works night and day to throw roadblocks in their way and to strap them with all kinds of regulations that make home schooling very difficult.

Brannon: *Finally, what advice would you give to concerned parents and grandparents as they fight to preserve and protect the values and beliefs of the traditional family?*

Mrs. Schlafly: I would say to join Eagle Forum and get together with people who have similar values so that you can participate in the political process and be effective — effective in electing candidates who will share your values; effective in lobbing for good legislation at the state and national level; effective in creating an atmosphere and a culture in which our views will be respected.

Brannon: *Thank you for your time and for what you are doing at Eagle Forum in helping to preserve the traditional family and their values.*

Chapter 1

[1]Lamar Alexander, quoted in *America 2000: An Education Strategy,* Texas Eagle Forum report by Cathie Adams, p. 1.

[2]*America 2000: An Education Strategy,* U.S. Department of Education, p. 19.

[3]Robert Morrison, "Business and Reform: A Golden Opportunity," *Family Policy,* Volume 4, Number 5, p. 5.

[4]Robert Morrison, "Americans Choosing Schools," *Family Policy,* Volume 4, Number 5.

[5]*Washington Post,* Feb. 21, 1992.

[6]Ibid.

[7]Morrison, "Americans Choosing Schools."

[8]*Washington Post,* Feb. 21, 1992.

[9]From a letter to the editor by Steven Marshall of Bound Brook, New Jersey.

[10]Ibid.

[11]William Buckley, *Tribune Review,* 1993.

[12]Dr. Brad Hayton, *America 2000: An Assessment* (Newport Beach, CA: Pacific Policy Institute, 1991).

[13]Phyllis Schlafly, quoted in the *Washington Post,* Feb. 21, 1992

[14]Hayton, *America 2000: An Assessment.*

Chapter 2

[1]Quote taken from video by Jeoffrey Botkin, *The Guiding Hand: The Clinton Influence on Arkansas Education,* 1993.

[2]Ibid.

[3]Ibid.

[4]Ibid.

[5]Ibid.

[6]Jeoffrey Botkin, quoted in private newsletter by Berit Kjos, "Clinton's Model School for New Age Education," January 1993.

[7]Ibid.

[8]Michael Kelly, "The New Year at a New Age Retreat," *New York Times* , Dec. 31, 1992. Quoted in newsletter by Berit Kjos, "Clinton's Model School for New Age Education."

[9]Dr. Thomas Sowell, "Revelations for the Anointed," *Forbes,* Jan. 18, 1992. Quoted in newsletter by Berit Kjos, "Clinton's Model School for New Age Education."

[10]Diane Ravitch, "Clinton's Math: More Gets Less," *The New York Times,* May 26, 1993.

[11]Bill & Nita Scoggan, "Say 'No' to Ted Kennedy," *The Beam,* Lighthouse Ministries, Aug. 1993.

[12]Ravitch, "Clinton's Math."

[13]Ibid.

[14]Ibid.

[15]*Washington Watch,* Family Research Council, May 11, 1993.

[16]Ibid.

[17]Ibid.

[18] Michael Swift. "America: Is This the Gay Declaration of War?"

[19]Article in *Arkansas Gazette,* July 3, 1988.

[20]*National Commission on Children* video, April 4, 1993.

[21]Baxter Bulletin, Oct. 4, 1991.

[22]*Washington Times,* July 14, 1993.

[23]Statistics supplied by the office of California Congressman Robert Dornan.

[24]Ibid.

[25]*West Memphis Evening Times,* July 14, 1993.

[26]Jane Pauley interview with Elders on "Dateline NBC," July 13, 1993.

[27]Information supplied by the office of Congressman Robert Dornan.

[28]*Arkansas Democrat Gazette,* Jan. 19, 1992.

[29]Douglas Groothuis, *Confronting the New Age* (Downers Grove, IL: InterVarsity Press, 1988), p. 129.

[30]*Washington Watch,* Family Research Council, May 1993.

[31]Barbera Vobejda, "Shalala: A Lifetime Spent in the Center of Storms," *Washington Post,* Jan. 14, 1993, p. A13.

Chapter 3

[1]Rush Limbaugh, *The Way Things Ought To Be* (New York, NY: Pocket Books, 1992), p. 150-151.

[2]Phyllis Schlafly, Copley News Service editorial, "NEA Antes Up to Defeat 'Choice'," *Greensburg Tribune Review,* Aug. 21, 1993.

[3]Ibid.

[4]Ibid.

[5]Ibid.

[6]Ibid.

[7]Ibid.

[8]Ibid.

[9]Ibid.

[10]"The National Education Association: Tearing Down American Values — At Your Expense," Special Report by NACE/CEE, Costa Mesa, CA, 1990.

[11]Ibid.

[12]Ibid.

[13]Ibid.

[14]Ibid.

[15]William Bennett, NBC's "This Week with David Brinkley," August 29, 1993.

[16]Ibid.

[17]Cal Thomas, "Net Tax Cut Could Prove Educational," *Greensburg Tribune Review,* Aug. 5, 1993.

[18]Ibid.

[19]Ibid.

[20]Ronald T. Bowes, "No Sin in Helping Parents Choose Schools with Religious Component," *Greensburg Tribune Review,* Aug. 8, 1993.

[21]Ibid.

[22]Ibid.

[23]Ibid.

[24]Leslie Ansley, "It Just Keeps Getting Worse," *USA Weekend,* Aug. 13-15, 1993, pp. 4-6.

[25]Bowes, "No Sin in Helping Parents."

[26]Ansley, "It Just Keeps Getting Worse."

[27]Ibid.

[28]Brannon Howse interview with the Honorable Jack Kemp. (See Appendix for complete interview.)

[29]Robert Morrison, "Americans Choosing Schools, " *Family Policy,* Volume 4, Number 5.

[30]ACSI Data, The Psychological Corporation, 1992.

[31]Henry Chur, *Los Angeles Times* article: "Revision in SAT Tests Give Students Headaches," *Greensburg Tribune Review,* Aug. 22, 1993.

[32]William J. Bennett, *Index of Leading Cultural Indicators* (Washington, DC: published jointly by Empower America, The Heritage Foundation, and Free Congress Foundation), Vol. 1, March 1993.

[33]Charles Murray, "What's Really Behind the SAT Score Decline?" *The Public Interest,* Winter 1992, No. 106.

[34]*Washington Watch,* Family Research Council, May 5, 1993.

[35]Phyllis Schlafly, Copley News Service editorial, "NEA Antes Up to Defeat 'Choice'," *Greensburg Tribune Review,* Aug. 21, 1993.

[36]Dr. Brad Hayton, *America 2000: An Assessment* (Newport Beach, CA: Pacific Policy Institute, 1991.

[37]William Bennett, *The Devaluing of America* (New York, NY: Summit Books, 1992), p. 62.

[38]George F. Will, "California Voters to Choose Who Gets a Choice in Schools," *Greensburg Tribune Review,* Aug. 27, 1993.

Chapter 4

[1]Kathy Simonds, *A Critique of America 2000, An Education Strategy,* Citizens for Excellence in Education, 1991, p. 30.

[2]Brannon Howse interview with Phyllis Schlafly. (See Appendix for complete interview.)

[3]Ibid.

[4]"America 2000: An Education Strategy," U.S. Department of Education, 1991, p. 32.

[5]Kathy Simonds, "A Critique of America 2000," Citizens for Excellence in Education, 1991, p. 30.

[6]Ibid.

[7]Simonds, p. 30-31.

[8]Ibid.

[9] Ibid., p. 30.

[10]Ibid., p. 31.

[11]*Insight,* March 1992, p. 8.

[12]Ibid., p. 4.

[13]Robert Morrison, *Americans Choosing Schools,* American Policy, Volume 4, Number 5.

[14]Katie Soffin, in a telephone interview with Brannon Howse on Feb. 16, 1993.

[15]*Washington Watch,* Family Research Council, May 1993.

[16]Ibid.

[17]Ibid.

[18]Laura Rogers, "The 'Parents as Teachers' Lives On," *Chronicles, In Loco Parentis, Part II,* Sept. 1992.

Chapter 5

[1]"A Nation at Risk," National Commission on Excellecne in Education, 1983, p. 7-8.

[2]Deborah A. Bentley, *Outcome Based Education: The Real Story?*, The Family Research Council, 1993, p.2.

[3]"Poor Results from Math Tests," *Education Reporter*, July 1991, Number 66.

[4]W.R. Daggett, *Preparing Students for the 190s and Beyond*, International Center for Leadership in Education, January 1992.

[5]Bentley, *Outcome Based Education*, p.15.

[6]Brannon Howse interview with Phyllis Schlafly. (See Appendix for complete interview.)

[7]*Education Week*, March 11, 1992.

[8]Bentley, *Outcome Based Education*, p.4.

[9]Ibid.

[10]C.P. Yecke, *St. Paul Pioneer Press*, June 1992.

[11]J.E. Roueche, "Can Mastery Learning Be Humane? The Case for Performance-Based Instruction," *Community College Review*, June 1975, Volume 3, no.4, p.14-21.

[12]William Bennet, *The Devauling of America* (New York, NY: Summit Books, 1992), p.57.

[13]Dr. S. Rimm, quoted in *Outcome Based Education: The Real Story?* by Deborah A. Bentley, 1993.

[14]C.P. Yecke, *OBE: The Work Ethic and Achievement*, Bulletin Publishing, Feb. 27, 1992.

[15]Taken from Linn-Mar, Iowa Community School District Guide to Student Progress, Grades K-4.

[16]Thomas Sowell, *Inside American Education* (New York, NY: The Free Press, 1992), p.2.

[17]Bennett, *The Devauling of America*, p.56.

[18]William Spady, *The Iowa Report a Special Report* (Des Moines, IA: Free World Research, Apr. 1993).

[19]Rick Schenker, "Why Don't We Just Get Back to Basics?" Pennsylvania Christian Coalition, Erie, PA.

Chapter 6

[1]*Education Weekly*, March 11, 1992.

[2]*The Senate Select Committee to Study the Michigan Model for Comprehensive School health Education*, December 1992, p.3.

[3]William Bennet, *The Devaluing of America* (New York, NY: Summit Books, 1992), p.58.

[4]*Senate Select Committe*, p.3.

[5]Ibid., p.12.

[6]Ibid., p.14.

[7]Ibid., p.16.

[8]Ibid., p.22.

[9]Ibid., p.23.

[10]Ibid., p.26.

[11]Ibid., p.27.

12Ibid., p.37.
13Information provided by the Family Research Council.
14Ibid.
15Ibid.

Chapter 7
1William J. Bennett and Edwin J. Delattre, *The Public Interest, Moral Education in the Schools*, The Heritage Foundation, 1978, p. 22.
2Ibid., p. 27.
3Ibid., p. 26.
4"Drug Prevention Curricula," U.S. Department of Education, 1988.
5Sidney Simon and Louis E. Raths, *Values Clarification* (Hart, 1978), p. 18.
6Richard A. Baer, Jr., "Parents, Schools, and Values Clarification," *Wall Street Journal*, April 12, 1982.
7From an interview with Rolf Zetterson.
8Bunny Hoest and John Reiner, "Laugh Parade," *USA Weekend*, August, 1993.
9Bennett and Delattre, *The Public Interest*, p. 56.
10Ibid.
11Constance Demborsky, *Personal and Social Responsibility*, Effective Skill Development for Adolescence, 1988, p. 46.
12Ibid., p. 63.
13"Jack and Jack and Jill and Jill," *Time*, December 14, 1992, p.52.
14"Teaching About Families That are Different," ABC News "Nightline" Transcript #2947, September 8, 1992.
15Ibid.
16*Focus on Family Newsletter*, June 1993, pp. 6-7.
17Howard Hurwitz, quoted in *USA Today*, January 12, 1993.
18 Ibid.
19"Teaching About Families That are Different," ABC News "Nightline" Transcript #2947, September 8, 1992.
20Brooks Alexander, "The Rise of Cosmic Humanism: What Is Religion?" *SCP Journal* (vol. 5, Winter 1981-82), p. 4.
21"Jack and Jack," p.52.
22 Tamara Henry, "Making Gays andLesbians Part of the Rainbow Curriculum," *USA Today*, January 12, 1993, p. 4d
23Richard John Neuhaus, "Belief Is in the Eye of the Beholder," *Religion and Society Report* (August 1986), p. 2.
24Rush Limbaugh, *The Way Things Ought To Be* (New York, NY: Pocket Books, 1992), p. 150.
25*The Rebirth of America*, Arthur S. Demoss Foundation, 1986, p. 82.

Chapter 8
1*Citizen Magazine*, July 20, 1992.
2Dr. James Dobson, "Where Do We Stand?" *Citizen Magazine*, June 1992.
3*Quest International* "Correct Responses," March 21, 1990.
4Ibid.
5Ibid.
6Dr. Harold M. Voth, in a letter to Mrs. Janice Rinks, Mt. Morris, MI.

[7]Dr. Joseph Adelson, in a letter to Prof. and Mrs. Robert Crown.

[8] William K. Kilpatrick, *Why Johnny Can't Tell Right from Wrong* (New York, NY: Simon & Schuster, 1992) p. 37.

[9]Brannon Howse interview with Phyllis Schlafly. (For complete interview see Appendix.)

[10]Quest International, *"Correct Response."*

[11]Dr. Adelson, letter to Rinks.

[12]*Drug Prevention Curricula: A Guide to Selection and Implementation.* Office of Educational Research and Improvement of the U.S. Department of Education, 1988, p. 43.

[13]From a report by Kathleen Honeycutt to the FLCC dated January 10, 1990.

[14]W.R. Coulson, Memorandum to Federal Drug Education Panel, April 23, 1988, p. 11.

[15]Concerned Women for America, August 1990, Volume 12 #8.

[16]Testimony given in hearing conducted by the United States Department of Education and included in a report titled, *Child Abuse in the Classroom,* edited by Phyllis Schlafly, pp. 61,99, 248, 398, 418.

[17]Ibid., p. 57.

[18]Ibid., p. 244.

[19]Ibid., p. 277.

[20]Vance Havner, *Playing Marbles with Diamonds* (Grand Rapids, MI: Baker Book House, 1985), p. 9.

[21]*National PTA's Guide to Extremism,* National Parent Teacher Association.

[22]Ibid.

[23]Ibid.

[24]Ibid.

[25]Gary Bauer quoted in *The Washington Post,* February 6, 1993.

[26]Ibid.

[27]*Focus on the Family Newsletter,* April 1993.

[28]Stephanie Chapman, "Campus Speech Codes are on the Way to Extinction," *Chicago Tribune,* July 9, 1992, p. 21.

[29]*National PTA's Guide to Extremism.*

[30]Carol Innerst, "Sensitivity is the Buzz Word at Colleges." *Washington Times,* August 29, 1990, page A1.

[31]Ibid.

[32]Dr. James Dobson and Gary Bauer, *Children at Risk* (Dallas, TX: Word Publishing, 1990), p. 209.

[33]*National PTA's Guide to Extremism.*

[34]Ibid.

[35]Paul Vitz, *Censorship: Evidence of Bias in Our Children's Textbooks* (Ann Arbor, MI: Servant, 1986), p.1.

[36]William J. Bennett, *The Devaluing of America* (New York, NY: Simon & Schuster, 1992), p. 58.

[37]Brannon Howse interview with Phyllis Schlafly.

[38]Ronald T. Bowes, "No Sin in Helping Parents Choose Schools with Religious Component," *Greensburg Tribune Review,* Aug. 8, 1993.

[39]Ibid.

Chapter 9

[1]Audrey Palm Riker and Charles Riker, *Finding My Way* (Ecino, CA: Bennett & McKnight, 1989).

[2]Ibid., p. 156.

[3]Ibid.

[4]Ibid.

[5]Ibid., p. 209.

[6]Ibid., p.224.

[7]Ibid.

[8]From a survey conducted by Mercer County Women's Action and Resource Center, Beulah, ND.

[9]Ibid.

[10]Thomas Sowell, *Inside American Education* (New York, NY: Free Press, 1993), p. 48.

[11]William K. Kilpatrick, *Why Johnny Can't Tell Right from Wrong* (New York, NY: Simon & Schuster, 1992), p. 48.

[12]Onalle McGraw, *Secular Humanism and the Schools: The Issue Whose Time Has Come*, The Heritage Foundation, 1976, p. 5.

[13]Kilpatrick, *Why Johnny Can't*, p. 22.

[14]Dana Mack, "What the Sex Educators Teach," *Commentary*, August 1993, p. 33.

[15]Ibid., p. 34.

[16] From a press release from Project Respect, February 3, 1993.

[17]Ibid.

[18]*Washington Watch*, Family Research Council, May 1993.

[19]Focus on the Family advertisement: "In Defense of a Little Virginity," 1993.

[20]Ibid.

[21]Ibid.

[22]Thomas Sowell, syndicated column, *New York Times*, 1992.

[23]Focus on the Family advertisement: "In Defense of a Little Virginity," 1993.

[24]Ronald T. Bowes, "No Sin in Helping Parents Choose Schools with Religious Component," *Greensburg Tribune Review*, August 8, 1993.

[25]Ibid.

[26]U.S. Dept. of Health & Human Services, Public Health Service, Centers for Disease Control, *1991 Division of STD/HIV Prevention*, Annual Report, p. 13, quoted in Focus on the Family advertisement: "In Defense of a Little Virginity," 1993.

[27]Bowes, *No Sin in Helping Parents.*

[28]Focus on the Family advertisement: "In Defense of a Little Virginity," 1993. (See Resource List to obtain information on how to get this ad printed in your local newspaper.)

Chapter 10

[1]John Dunphy, *The Humanist Magazine*, Jan./Feb., 1983, p. 26.

[2]Robert Morrison, "Americans Choosing Schools," *Family Policy*, Volume 4, Number 5, p. 6-7.

[3]Brooks Alexander, "The Rise of Cosmic Humanism: What is Religion?" *SCP Journal* (Vol. 5, winter 1981-82), p.4.

[4]Dunphy, *The Humanist.*

[5]Marilyn Ferguson, *The Aquarian Conspiracy* (Los Angeles, CA: J.P. Tarcher, 1980), p. 280.

[6]*Saturday Education,* March 1973.

[7]Thomas Sowell, *Inside American Education* (New York, NY: Free Press, 1993), p.48.

[8]Ibid.

[9]Ibid., p. 51.

[10]Ibid., p. 50.

[11]Ibid.

[12]William Bennett, *The Devaluing of America* (New York, NY: Summit Books, 1992), p.48.

[13]Ibid.

[14]Ibid.

[15]Gary Kah, *En Route to Global Occupation,* (Lafayette, LA: Huntington House, 1992), p. 59.

[16]Ibid.

[17]Ibid., p. 60.

[18]Bennett, *The Devaluing of America,* p. 45.

[19]Kah, *En Route to Global Occupation,* p. 61.

[20]Ibid., p. 60.

[21]Ibid., p. 61.

[22]Ibid.

[23]Ibid.

[24]Bennett, *The Devaluing of America,* p. 49.

[25]Ibid.

[26]Taken from a TV/radio interview, Channel 6, Omaha, Nebraska, with Congressman Hoagland.

[27]1983, *The Mel Gablers Newsletter,* Published by National Association of Christian Educators, Costa Mesa, CA.

Chapter 11
[1]*Impressions* (Harcourt, Brace, and Jovanovich).

[2]Thomas Jensen's review of the *Impressions* series.

[3]President's Report, *Citizens for Excellence in Education,* June 1990.

[4]*Citizen Magazine,* February 18, 1991, p. 2.

[5]Ibid., p. 4.

[6]Ibid., p. 4.

[7]Ibid., p. 3.

[8]Ibid., p. 3.

[9]A review of *Impressions* by Clinical Psychologist Scott Voss, January 27, 1992.

[10]Jensen, review of *Impressions.*

[11]Ibid.

[12]Ibid.

[13]*Citizen Magazine,* February 18, 1991, p. 5.

[14]Jensen, review of *Impressions.*

[15]Ibid.

[16]Ibid.

Chapter 12

[1]"More Kafka than Capra," by David Brooks, *National Review*, September 30, 1988, p. 29.

[2]*Index of Leading Cultural Indicators*, published Jointly by Empower America, The Heritage Foundation, and Free Congress Foundation, Volume 1, March 1993.

[3]Ibid.

[4]Michael Medved, *Hollywood v. America: Popular Culture and the War on Values* (Harper Collins, 1992) quoted in *Index of Leading Cultural Indicators*.

[5]Ibid.

[6]Dr. James Dobson and Gary Bauer, *Children at Risk* (Dallas, TX: Word Publishing, 1990), p. 208.

[7]*Focus on the Family Newsletter*, June 1992.

[8]John H. Court, "The Family and Hollywood," *The Rebirth of America*, Arthur S. DeMoss Foundation, 1986.

[9]According to Michael Medved in an interview conducted by KTIS FM Minneapolis/St. Paul.

[10]William Bennett, *The Devaluing of America* (New York, NY: Summit Books, 1992), p. 34.

[11]Dobson and Bauer, *Children at Risk*.

[12]Medved, quoted in *Rush Limbaugh Newsletter*, February 1993.

[13]Ibid., p. 2.

[14]Medved, quote in *Rush Limbaugh Newsletter*.

[15]According to Michael Medved in an interview conducted by KTIS FM Minneapolis/St. Paul.

[16]*Rush Limbaugh Newsletter*, February 1993, p. 3.

[17]Ibid., p. 4.

[18]*Focus on the Family Newsletter*, June 1992.

[19]*Rush Limbaugh Newsletter*, p. 4.

[20]*Focus on the Family Newsletter*, June 1992.

[21]*Time*, July 29, 1991, p. 60.

[22]Ibid.

[23]Ibid.

[24]Ibid.

[25]Ibid.

[26]Dave Hunt, *CIB Bulletin*.

[27]Ibid., p. 21.

[28]Terry Mattingly, "My Daughter Loves to Watch Teenage Mutant Ninja Turtles," 1992.

[29]Ted Turner quoted in *AFA Journal*, October 1989.

[30]Rick McGough, *One Minute Till Midnight*, (Moline, IL: New Life Fellowship Assembly of God, 1988).

[31]Ted Turner quoted in an article from the *Denver Post*.

Chapter 13
[1]Brannon S. Howse, *The New Age Is Not So New* (St. Paul, MN: Concept of Truth, 1990), p. 13.
[2]*U.S. News and World Report,* May 1983 supplement.
[3]*Revelation: Growth Through Discovery Bible Study Series* (Mpls./St. Paul, MN: Growth Through Discovery Ministries, 1988).
[4] *Futurist Magazine,* March-April 1987, pp. 10-11.
[5]*Revelation: Growth.*
[6]Arthur C. Clark, *July 20, 2019, Life in the 21st Century* (New York, NY: McMillian Publishing), 1986, p. 275, 276.
[7]Gary Kah, *En Route to Global Occupation* (Lafayette, LA: Huntington House, 1992), p. 37.
[8]John Whitehead, *The End of Man* (Macon, GA:Good News, 1986).
[9]Stephen Holley and Macol Hash, *Looking for That Blessed Hope* (St. Paul, MN: Concepts of Truth, 1993) p. 36.
[10]Rick McGough, *One Minute Till Midnight* (Moline, IL: New Life Fellowship Assembly of God, 1988).
[11]Ibid.
[12]Ibid.
[13]Dave Burnham, *The Rise of the Computer State* (New York, NY: Randam, 1983).
[14]*Futurist,* July-Aug. 1989.
[15]*Revelation: Growth.*
[16]Ibid.
[17]Ibid.
[18]Ibid.
[19]Ibid.
[20]Holley & Hash, *Looking for That Blessed Hope,* p. 36.
[21]Vance Havner, *Playing Marbles with Diamonds* (Grand Rapids, MI: Baker Book House, 1985), p. 90.
[22]Ibid., p. 57.
[23]Dave Hunt, *CIB Bulletin.*
[24]Havner, *Playing Marbles,* p. 65.

Chapter 14
[1]*St. Paul Pioneer Press,* April 29, 1992.
[2]Vance Havner, *Playing Marbles with Diamonds* (Grand Rapids, MI: Baker Book House, 1985), p. 63.
[3]Charles R. Swindoll, *Come Before Winter and Share My Hope* (Wheaton, IL: Tyndell House Publishers, 1985), p. 113.
[4]From a sermon by Richard Reynertson, Fairmont, MN, Bethel Evangelical Free Church.

Resource List

Thomas Sowell, *Inside American Education* (New York, NY: Free Press, 1993).

William Bennett, *The Devaluing of America* (New York, NY: Summit Books, 1992).

William Kilpatrick, *Why Johnny Can't Tell Right from Wrong* (New York, NY: Simon & Schuster, 1992).

Gary Kah, *En Route to Global Occupation* (Lafayette, LA: Huntington House Publishers, 1992).

Vance Havner, *Playing Marbles with Diamonds* (Grand Rapids, MI: Baker Book House, 1985).

Jeffrey Botkin "Clinton's Governor's School" video, $19.95, 1-800-886-8852.

The New Age Is Not So New — Video

This is a 90-minute professionally produced and packaged video on the New Age movement and how it is affecting the traditional family. This video, with all its graphics, makes it easy to see how the philosophies of the New Age movement touches all facets of life including education, media, the American corporation, and the church. Recorded while Brannon Howse was live in seminar. $20.00 plus S & H.

Concepts of Truth — Monthly newsletter

If you enjoyed Brannon's book you will really appreciate his monthly publication entitled *Concepts of Truth*. This monthly newsletter takes an honest straightforward look at the current issues that are affecting today's traditional family. For just $20.00 a year you will receive 12 issues of *Concepts of Truth*. Through this monthly publication you will be kept up to date on important pending legislation. You will receive the information you need to take action to see that harmful bills are defeated, as well as how to aid in the passage of bills that will strengthen the American family. This informative newsletter looks at issues that are of concern to all of us from education, film, and television, and issues confronting today's church and family. Don't depend on the newspapers and news reporters to keep you informed. *Concepts of Truth* tells you what they will not.

For booking inquiries, please call or write to:

Brannon Howse Ministries
P.O. Box 25062
St. Paul, MN 55125
(612) 739-4112

Cradle to College

The Video

If you have enjoyed this book, you will certainly appreciate Brannon's 77-minute informative video by the same title. *Cradle to College,* the video, is a professionally packaged and produced video presentation. This video, hosted by Brannon Howse, covers such important topics as The Indoctrination in Education, Outcome-Based Education, America/Goals 2000, the Parents as Teachers Program, values clarification, and the curriculum in the classroom.

State of the art graphics and pictures aid in the understanding of these important issues. This video is a must for all concerned parents and educators. Don't wait — order today and share this important information with your friends. The cost of the vidceo is just $19.95, plus $3.00 shipping and handling.

To order by mail:

Brannon Howse Ministries
P.O. Box 25062
St. Paul, MN 55125

To order with your VISA or MasterCard:

1-800-444-BOOK
(1-800-444-2665)

About the author . . .

Brannon is the president of Brannon Howse Ministries and resides in Minneapolis/St. Paul with his wife, Melissa. Brannon was born in Jackson, Mississippi, and then moved with his family to live for ten years in Fairfax, Virginia, just outside of Washington, DC. Brannon has made Minnesota his home for the past ten years.

Following his studies as a classical tenor, Brannon began traveling the country, ministering in some of the nation's largest churches and convention halls. It was through Brannon's travels that he discovered the need to alert the church to the dangers of the New Age movement. Brannon wrote and published the first curriculum and media kit ever published on the New Age movement entitled, "The New Age Is Not So New."

Brannon now travels to 40-45 churches a year, preaching on Sunday morning, ministering in concert on Sunday evening, and conducting his three-hour, four-color, multi-media seminar on Monday evenings, entitled, "The Traditional Family's Quest for Survival." Brannon is also a well sought after convention speaker to present not only his seminar on the family, but also his presentation based on his book *Cradle to College.*